Creating Your First Novel

A comprehensive guide spanning the entire long-term project: from planning through marketing and starting your author business.

By Hank Quense

Other nonfiction books by Hank Quense
Creating Stories
Book Marketing Fundamentals
Self-publish A Book In 10 Steps
Infographic Guide to Creating Stories
How To Self-publish And Market A Book
Business Basics For Authors
Infographic Guide To Mind-mapping A Novel
Fiction Writing Insights
Book Marketing Insights
Self-publishing Insights
Author Business Insights
SWOT Insights

All Rights Reserved

License Notes

No part of this book may be reproduced, stored in a retrieval system, or transmitted in any format or by any means without express written consent from the publisher. This book may not be resold or redistributed in any manner without express written permission from the publisher.

ISBN:9798985309799

Published in the United States of America.
Published by Strange Worlds Publishing.

Main Table of Contents

Foreword   7
Planning.   11
Writing.   14
Author business   64
Publishing   89
Marketing   130
Index   156
About the author   163

Foreword

The Problem

Creating a novel is an awesome achievement, but it isn't achieved without a lot of effort and that effort is expended over a lengthy period of time. Many authors, when creating their first book, don't appreciate that they are getting into a multi-phase, long-term project.

This project can be outlined this way and is the same for a novel or a nonfiction book.

Phase 1: Planning the book
Phase 2: Writing the book
Phase 3: Publishing the book
Phase 4: Marketing the book
Phase 5: Managing a business

What each phase involves is explained below.

Phase 1: Planning: For a novel, this activity is called Story Design. It's where you embed all your creative ideas into the story elements such as characters, plots, settings. For a nonfiction book, the planning mostly involves research, sometimes extensive research, and organizing that research into a logical order.

Phase 2: Writing: In this phase you spend your time banging on the key board and cursing at the screen or staring out a window.

Phase 3: Publishing: These days an author has options to chose from. These range from the traditional way involving an agent and a publisher to self-publishing with several options in between.

Phase 4: Marketing: No matter how the book is published most, if not all, of the marketing responsibility falls on the author.

Phase 5: The business: After all this activity, many authors are shocked to discover they now own a business. This sudden promotion to CEO of a business whose objective is to market and sell the book can be upsetting.

Another facet of reality is that writing the book does nothing to prepare the author for the daunting tasks of publishing, marketing and organizing a business. The usual remedy is to do a lot of research and/or studying as each phase of the project unfolds. Too many times, the next phase is a surprise to the author.

There has to be a better way!

The Solution

I've written over 30 books, most of them self-published. I've stumbled through all of the phases listed above a few times before I mastered the process. Recently, I decide to develop a thorough explanation of all the phases in a comprehensive way that would save new authors from experiencing the frustration of trying to figure out each phase as it unfolds.

The initial part of the project involved whiteboards instead of books. This took a bit of time and the whiteboards became quite expansive. Over all, the whiteboards have in excess of 475 cards with each card containing a piece of information such as text, video or a downloadable file. I used the Scrintal app as the software to develop these whiteboards and I ended with a total of eight of them. You can find the master whiteboard with links to the other whiteboards here: https://beta.scrintal.com/b/author-ecosystem-master-board--bnrgc

I also rearranged the phases this way:

Phase 1: Planning the book
Phase 2: Writing the book
Phase 3: Starting the author business
Phase 4: Publishing the book
Phase 5: Marketing the book.

One of the principle objectives in this project was to arm the new author with the information needed to understand the entire scope of creating a new book. In other words, I wanted to eliminate surprises for the author.

Understanding the scope of the entire project has an interesting side-effect; it lessens the possibility that the new author will fall prey to scam artists. These scammers prowl the web searching for such authors and 'offer' to help them. The reality is that their 'help' is only aimed at emptying the author's wallet or purse.

In this revised arrangement, the author starts the business after the manuscript has been completed and is getting worked over by an editor.

While whiteboards are a great way to display vast amounts of information visually, unfortunately, they have a very limited exposure. You can't, for instance, put the whiteboards on Amazon where everybody can find them.

This conclusion led me to decide to use the whiteboards as models for a series of short ebooks packaged under a single title.

My objective with all this work is to simplify the job of the new author by explaining the complicated process of creating a book. Along the way, the first book devolved to simply Planning.

You'll need a notebook of some sort to jot notes as you go along with this book. By the time you finish reading this book, you'll have written a lot of notes and detailed other useful information.

The Fiction Writing Workshop is for those aspiring authors who want to write a novel but aren't sure how to start it or how to write it. The workshop will provide valuable lessons (and assignments) on how to go about constructing the story.

The short books listed above were created one at a time. For a brief period, I thought about publishing them as individual books, but that represented a waste of resources and money. The series would require a lot of ISBNs, covers, etc. For economic reasons, I decided to package the series into a single book. This plan has a slight disadvantage since each book was written to be.a complete stand-alone product: consequently, there are duplications. In other words, you'll sometimes read the same content in different parts of this book.

This book is part of an author ecosystem I've been creating. Another part of the ecosystem is my website called Writers & Authors Resource Center or WritersARC. The link to this website is:
    https://hankquense.podia.com/

Hank Quense
Westwood, NJ

Planning

Fiction Planning

This type of planning is often called story design. It's where you embed all your creative ideas into the story elements such as characters, plots, setting and so forth. I spend a considerable amount of time on story design before I start to write the first draft. A notebook will come in handy to jot down notes and ideas as you go through the material in this book.

Initial Details

The details below are basic and necessary and should be kept in a notebook or a file. All the information will probably change over time.

Working title:
Theme:
Brief Storyline:
Co-authors (if any):

Outline

Use your notebook to develop an outline for your story. This outline will become the basis for the synopsis that you will have to write eventually. You won't be able to complete it right away. It will grow over time as you develop more ideas.

Cast of characters

Use this list to identify the main characters in the story. For characters who are not the hero and the bad guy, denote the character's role. Examples are mother-in-law, drug dealer, sidekick, etc. Expand as needed. This list can take up several pages in your notebook.

Protagonist:
Antagonist:
Character 1:
Character 2:
Character 3:
Character 4:

Character 5:

Character Development
Stories are about characters. Character development involves several specific areas: physical attributes, biography and mental attributes. Much of your planning time will be spent in developing the main characters in the story.

Plot
A typical plot consists of the protagonist recognizing the plot problem and failing three times to solve the problem. A final do-or-die attempt follows. This sequence is shown below.

Typical plot sequence
Inciting event
First failure
Second failure
Third failure
Climax (do-or-die attempt)
Validation scene

Setting
Setting can do much more than describe the backdrop for the story. It should convey and define the time period and the location(s).

There are two types of settings in a story: the overall story setting and the scene setting. The scene settings are all subsets of the story setting.

Example: your story is set in the Sahara Desert. Scene settings can be an oasis, a fort, sand dunes, a sand storm and more.

In your notebook, briefly describe the setting of your story:
List as many potential scene settings as you can think of.

World building
If your story is sci-fi or fantasy, you'll have to give your readers some ideas on what the world looks like. The same is true if your story takes place in another era.

Note: this information is different from the story's setting.

World building can be a complicated undertaking. Below are several links to websites that contain information on this topic:

https://www.youtube.com/watch?v=JgHI5f7hbIw&t=4s
https://jerryjenkins.com/worldbuilding/
https://www.masterclass.com/articles/how-to-write-a-believable-world

But, what if . . .

When I'm working on a new book, I frequently play what-if with the characters or the plot or the storyline. This (not always) leads to exciting developments that strengthen the story. Sometimes, it leads to confusion that has to be sorted out.

Use your notebook to engage in what-if's in your story. Examples: What if character A is gay? What if character B isn't a serial killer but is something entirely different? What if the story takes place on a large asteroid instead of Mars? What if at the climax the town is cut off by an earthquake.

After the initial what-if statement, work on the logical conclusion to the what if.

What if 1:
What if 2:
What if 3:
What if 4:
What if 5:
What if 6:

Fiction Writing Workshop

Workshop Table of Contents

Lesson 1: Getting started.   14
Lesson 2: Setting.   18
Lesson 3: Character development.   21
Lesson 4: Character arc.   27
Lesson 5: Plots.   29
Lesson 6: Subplots.   35
Lesson 7: Scene design.   39
Lesson 8: Emotional arc   42
Lesson 9: Point of view.   47
Lesson 10: Story-telling techniques.   52
Lesson 11: Dialog.   56
Lesson 12: Assorted topics.   58
Lesson 13: Wrapping it all up.   62

Lesson 1: Getting Started

Target audience

This workshop is aimed at people who want to write a story but don't know how or even where to start.

I think the minimum age to use the workshop is 7th grade, but there will always be exceptions.

Ideas

Before we get too far, I want to say a few words about ideas.

You need a way to jot down your ideas. Once you get into this project, ideas will come at you at all times of the day where ever you are. If you don't write them down, they will be lost. Your note doesn't have to be with a pen and paper. It can be a voice memo on your phone or a note in a digital notebook.

Writing prompts

Let's get started.

I'm going to give you a writing prompt. Using a notebook or your computer, start writing about whatever jumps into your mind. Don't overthink it. Just write for five minutes then stop and come back here.

Prompt: A*t the post office*.

Time's up. Since you aren't a writer (yet) , you probably used your speaking voice for what you wrote. As a writer, you have to develop a writing voice to use when you write. Why? Because our speaking voice is terrible to read.

It's loaded with:
- Was & were sentences, adverbs, -ing words.
- Empty words: very, even, ever, really, still, just, then.
- Pronouns instead of proper names

Practice

For the next few minutes rewrite what you have and get rid of as many 'was' and 'were' uses and empty words as you can.

If you want to be a writer, you have to write. Every day. It's best if you do it at the same time. To help you get into the habit, use one of these prompts every day for a week. Afterwards, rewrite to eliminate the speaking voice.

Day 1: at the post office

Day 2: an oak tree

Day 3: driving on the Turnpike

Day 4: Penn Station

Day 5: overdue at the library

Day 6: my favorite movie

Day 7: I hate ????

Story definition

So, what is a story? Let's agree on a definition. I like these two definitions by two different and very prolific authors.

A story is a narrative description of a character struggling to solve a problem. Nothing more than that. And nothing less. Ben Bova, The Craft of Writing Science Fiction.

A story consists of a character in a context with a problem. Based on Algis Budrys's book Writing to the Point.

Both of these statements say essentially the same thing. The key elements are: character, struggle, problem, context (setting).

I find it interesting that the definitions say "story" but don't mention what type of story, such as a novel or a script. The reason for that is that the type of story is irrelevant. A story is a story. The definition applies to any and all types of stories since all types of stories require characters, plots, setting, scenes and other elements.

Story ideas

A story idea can be about a character, a problem, a setting or something else.

Story ideas are all around you. You just have to look for them.

You need to come up with a few of these because a single story idea may not make it. Only about 10% of your story ideas will actually work out. Or less.

How many words?

This is a popular question. The popular answer is "As many words as it takes to tell the story." I find this answer factitious. It should also say "unless that many words violate the submission guidelines."

In my opinion, a short story is just that: short. It should be five thousand words or less. Certainly six thousand words is the outer limit. Novels average about eighty thousand words. If you are submitting a short story or a longer work to a publisher, it will have word count guidelines on its website.

So what do you do if your word count exceeds the guidelines? Another reason the answer above is factitious is that it implies the word count necessary to tell the story is an absolute value. That is completely false.

Stories can be engineered to meet word count guidelines. If the story is too long, there are a number of ways to lower the word count. Eliminate a main character. Eliminate a subplot. Start the story further into the story time.

If you want to increase the word count without simply padding the text with unnecessary words, there are other strategies you can employ. Add a main character or subplot or start the story earlier.

In other words, story length is fungible and adaptable.

Assignment 1

In your notebook, come up with at least three story ideas.

For each idea, write a few sentences to expand the idea into something more substantial. This will make the idea more tangible to you, especially when you look at the idea six months from now.

Lesson 2: Setting

Imagery

Reading a story involves building images in your mind. Your brain takes the author's words and uses them to develop images of what's going on in the story. In this way, the reader creates an image of the setting for a scene or what a character looks like.

What this means is the writer has a duty to provide the reader with the proper image building words or the story will fail for the reader. In other words, you need to provide descriptions because reading involves using your brain.

Why is this important? Look at the cartoon.

This is the difference between reading and watching.

Watching TV and movies is essentially brainless. You can shut off your brain because you see and hear everything you have to know.

Reading involves using your brain. Readers have to build images from the author's words.

This is an important concept that should be in the forefront of your mind whenever you are working on the book.

Setting

Image building starts with the story's setting.

Setting can do much more than describe the backdrop for the story. It should convey and define the time period and that defines the customs of the characters. It can set up the reader's expectations about the type of story he is about to read.

Example: character leaning against a wall.
- In a dark, dingy alley
- In a spaceship
- In a castle

Obviously, the reader will expect different types of stories with each opening.

There are two types of setting: story and scenes.

Story setting: The town or city where you live.

Scene settings: Library, train station, a tavern, hospital, ball field, school.

The story setting imposes limitations: you can't write whatever you feel like writing.

For instance, if your story is set in ancient Rome, you can't have characters with knowledge of advanced mathematics or using pistols.

In a short story, the setting should be established in the first few paragraphs. In a novel, in the opening chapter.

The setting used in your story has to be accurate. Don't try to set a story in Manhattan's Central Park if you haven't been there or unless you have thoroughly researched it on the internet.. Likewise, the French Quarter in New Orleans is unique and shouldn't be used by anyone who hasn't walked the narrow streets or properly researched it.

An effect of establishing the setting is the placing of limitations on the author and the characters. For the author, a space ship means he shouldn't have the characters using swords and landline phones since these artifacts are from bygone eras.

Your characters are also limited. A character in the Old West can't have knowledge of computers or smartphones unless he's a time-traveler.

If you write a story that uses weapons from a different era or knowledge not available at that time, you'd better have a good reason why it makes sense. You don't have to convince yourself, you have to convince the reader.

Assignment 2
Where does your story take place?
Describe it in a paragraph or two.
Now identify locations that can be used for scenes to take place.

Lesson 3: Character development

Characters

The story definition you saw earlier said stories are about characters

A character can be almost anything: a human, a fantasy creature, an alien, an animal, an inanimate object like a rock or a car. Whatever it is, the character must be capable of talking and experiencing emotions.

A short story needs three characters: a protagonist (hero), an antagonist (bad guy) and a sidekick for the hero. Start thinking about these characters as we go through the meeting's content.

Developing characters takes time, a lot of time. You probably won't finish the development at once. My characters tend to be developed over time as I come up with more ideas about the character.

A major character needs development in four separate areas:
- Physical attributes
- Mental attributes
- Biography
- Dominant reader emotion

A minor character needs less development. Physical attributes may be sufficient.

Physical attributes

Besides the usual stuff, give the character some unique identifier. Examples are: a lisp, a scar, a tattoo. The main purpose of the physical attributes is to allow the reader to build an image of the character.

This also establishes limitations on what the character is capable of doing. A weak, scrawny character can't pick up heavy objects and throw them.

The way a character moves can be a good way of differentiating him from other characters. Your character can walk with a limp or use a cane. Other movement options are walking faster or slower than others.

Does your character talk with a lisp? Does she stutter? Does she pepper her speech with foreign words? These bits of development can be used to make a character different from others.

A facial scar is a defining trait. So is a tattoo. Birthmarks or skin discoloration also fall into this category.

If you decide your character limps or has a scar, make sure your biographical material covers what happened to the character. How did the character get the limp or scar?

Biography

A biography for the character serves a dual purpose. Besides providing background information, it allows the author to understand the character, and that understanding is vital when dealing with the character in stressful situations.

The strange thing to many new story writers is this: most of the biographical material won't show up in the story, so why bother developing it? The answer is that the bio allows the writer to understand the character and what makes him or her tick. The better the writer knows and understands the character, the better the writer will be able to predict how the character will respond to situations and stimuli.

Example:

Suppose someone walks up to your character and punches him in the mouth, or a beautiful woman kisses him. How does your character react to the punch? Does he punch back? Does he walk away?

How does the character react to the kiss? Does he get red in the face? Does he kiss her back? Does he develop a stammer? Does he ask for her phone number?

Your detailed biography and the mental attributes will guide you in writing the character's response. If you don't have the bio material, the character's response is really a guess.

If the character was always getting in fights in school, he'll probably punch back. If the character is shy, he'll get red in the face.

There are a number of biographical elements the writer should address.

Family: Are his parents alive? Does the character have any siblings? What is everyone's age? Are any siblings married? Where did the character grow up? Did the character have any unusual childhood experiences? What were they? Do these experiences affect the character? Is the character's family stable? Or is it chaotic? How does this affect him?

Education: Schools, degrees, favorite subject?

Career: Jobs, military experience?

Adult experiences: Married? Divorced? Children?

It's the author's job to come up with events that will affect the character's life and outlook.

Mental attributes

These make your character real.

Nothing tells the reader the author is an amateur more quickly than reading about a make-believe cardboard character, one that isn't a "real" person. As you develop this part of your character you will, once again, run into the limitation factor. The more defined your character becomes, the more limitations you'll place on the character and yourself.

Personality:

Your main characters need to have a personality. Here are links to sites that describe what this means.

http://www.16personalities.com/personality-types

http://examples.yourdictionary.com/examples-of-personality-traits.html

Once you establish this character trait, you will be forced to have the character act, think and talk in accordance with that trait. Readers will instantly smoke out deviations.

Dreams

What does your character want out of life? What does he want to be when he grows up?

This attribute can influence how the character acts and can provide a measure of conflict. What if she wants to become an engineer but has to decide whether to stay in college or drop out to help her sick mother? This situation will provide inner conflict which readers love.

Memories

These are influencers that characters have. Memories can also be used for foreshadowing and to build up internal conflict. How? Consider this example: as a five-year-old, the character almost drowned. Ever since, she has had a healthy fear of open water. At some point in the story, she sees a man drowning in the middle of a lake. What does your character do? Does her fear of water cause her to ignore the man and walk away? Does she search for a boat to use in the rescue? Does she suppress her fear and dive into the lake?

This inner conflict can provide a memorable scene in the story. Remember, a heroine has to do heroic stuff. It would be acceptable for a villainess to let the guy drown, but a heroine will have to try to save him, or she won't be believable. If she lets the guy drown without trying to save him, the character will be seen as a phony and the reader will lose interest in her.

Mirages

These are fantasies the character tricks herself into believing. Want an example? Most politicians who think they have the slightest chance of getting elected President. Chasing a mirage can be an entire short story. Or a sub-plot in a novel.

Philosophy

Everyone has a personal philosophy. You have one whether you realize it or not, whether you want one or not.

Here are a few to get you started:
- Individualism: Philosophical theory emphasizing personal freedom and autonomy.
- Idealism: Theory that reality is a creation of the mind, and that mental and spiritual values, rather than matter, constitute reality; immaterialism.
- Optimism: Doctrine holding that reality is fundamentally good and the world is governed by benign forces.
- Pessimism: Reality is fundamentally evil and the world is governed by malevolent forces.
- Pragmatism: Emphasizes consequences and practical results of one's conduct rather than principles and categories of reality.

Give each of your characters a philosophy.

This attribute establishes a limitation. For example, optimists and pessimists will act very differently from each other.

Dominant reader emotion

This isn't part of the character's inner or outer aspects. It also isn't part of the character's biography, but it is a very important aspect of the character.

The Dominant Reader Emotion (DRE) is the emotion you want (hope!) the reader will experience whenever the character is in a scene. There are a number of reader emotions you can use. Typical emotions are: admiration sympathy, pity, dislike, annoyance and many more.

Whatever reader emotion you choose dictates the way you write about the character and limits what you can have the character do. For example, if you wish the reader to 'like' a character, you can't have that character kicking puppies or pushing little old ladies in front of buses. You can have a character do these things if the reader emotion you're striving for is anger or disgust.

This is one of the first things I assign when developing a new character because it affects other character attributes. Suppose you give a character the DRE of admiration, how are you going to develop this character?

Antagonist development

Naturally, writers spend a great deal of time developing the protagonist for their stories. After all, this character is the star of the story. But for the protagonist to really shine, he has to contend with a well-developed antagonist. In a nutshell, that means the writer has to spend time developing a bad guy who is as interesting as the good guy.

It may come as a surprise to some that the bad guy doesn't have to be 'bad.' The antagonist can be just as moral, dedicated and upright as the good guy. Nevertheless, the antagonist has to strive to defeat the protagonist or to keep the good guy from succeeding.

Here is an example to explain this conundrum. Suppose the world is threatened by pollution or an alien invasion. Both character A (the protagonist) and character B (the antagonist) develop plans to save the world. A thinks B's plan is terrible and will only serve to increase the danger. B thinks the same thing about A's plan. So the conflict here is between A and B as they strive to have their plans accepted and implemented. Notice that both have the same goal: to save the world. Their only difference concerns how to go about saving the world.

To be sure, many antagonists are not nice guys. There are a number of types of villainy possible. You should select one and develop the antagonist accordingly.

Here is a list of villain types. This is based on the ebook *Writing About Villains* by Rayne Hall.

- The Evil Overlord is at the top of a power pyramid and wants still more power.
- The Schemer fits into any society and plans for the long term.
- The Obsessed Scientist is intelligent, analytical, creative and determined.
- The Smothering Mother dominates her family or community or club.
- The Fanatic is motivated by deeply held, often religious convictions.
- The Seductress uses her charms (either her mind or body) to get what she wants.
- The Sadist's motivation is pleasure at the victim's pain or fear.
- The Confidence Trickster is good at reading people, adaptable, confident, persuasive, inspiring.
- The Social Reject stands outside society. He may be an outlaw, a nerd or misfit.
- The Bully picks on vulnerable victims, motivated by the short-term power boost his ego gets.

Once you assign the villain type, make sure your character development supports that type of villain.

Assignment 3

Begin the development of the characters for your story.

A short story will require at least three characters while novel can have an unlimited number of character

Lesson 4: Character arc

Character arc

In this lesson, I'll go over a very important part of creating a story: the character arc.

Every story needs a character arc. Basically, there are two types. One concerns itself with what great lesson the main character learns over the course of the story. The second is what changes in the life of that character as a result of the events in the story.

If there is no character arc, then everything after the story ends is the same as before the story began. In other words, nothing happened. The only thing that changed is that the characters got older.

A story without a character arc is an incomplete and unsatisfactory story.

The character arc can be physical or mental or both, but a mental character arc is more interesting than a physical one. In a mental character arc, the character learns an important lesson. In a physical one, the character's situation changes for better, or for worse.

A character arc isn't an on-off switch. It's a story-within-a-story.

Examples

To get a deeper understanding of character arcs, we can look at a few examples.

A character starts out as a bigot, but during the course of the story learns to be less bigoted and becomes more open-minded.

Another example concerns itself with a proud or pompous (or both) character who gets humbled as the story unfolds.

A lazy character gets motivated.

A character evolves from an uninterested bystander or a follower into the leader of a movement.

From the movies:

In Star Wars, Luke Skywalker evolves from a rustic farm boy into a Jedi knight (and it only took three movies for that to happen).

In Lord of the Rings, both the books and the movies, Frodo evolves. As a result of his journey, he changes from an inexperienced youth to a strong-minded, decisive man (or hobbit, to be more precise).

Assignment 4

You need a character arc for your protagonist. You can give your bad guy a character arc also but that is optional.

Describe the character arc your protagonist will experience. Write a paragraph or two on how the character changes over the course of the story.

Lesson 5: Plots

Plots

What does a plot do? It gives the characters a job! Until your story has a plot, the characters are just hanging around doing nothing.

The plot stretches the entire length of the story from the inciting incident to the climax.

Developing a plot requires a lot of creativity and thinking. You may not be able to complete it right away. I have story ideas from years ago that I haven't been able to construct a plot for. The sticking point is this: The plot you build must be one that YOU believe in. If you don't, you'll never be able to convince the reader to believe in it.

Plot problem

The first step in the plot building process is to come up with the plot problem. Just what is the hero supposed to be doing or fixing. Now is a good time to come up with a potential plot problem. Or two. Or three. Just in case the first one doesn't work out.

And while you're at it, come up with the hero's motivation. Why does the protagonist want to solve the problem? Why doesn't she (or he or it) say "Screw this. I'm too busy," or "I ain't doing this." This is a vital step in establishing the believability of the story and the character. Without this proper motivation, the reader will never buy into the story.

And why does the bad guy oppose the hero? The antagonist also needs proper motivation that is equal in strength to the hero's motivation.

Bad news

The second step in building the plot is to come up with the ending. Yeah, that's right. You need to know the ending. Right now!

Why? Because you have to develop a path that consists of plot events that will take the reader on a journey from the inciting incident to the climax.

The inciting incident is where the hero finds out about the plot problem.
The climax is the plot ending.
You can't develop the plot path unless you know where it has to go.
That's why you need the ending before you go any further.

Plot cloud
Let's talk about why completing a plot path is so difficult.
This diagram is the plot cloud:

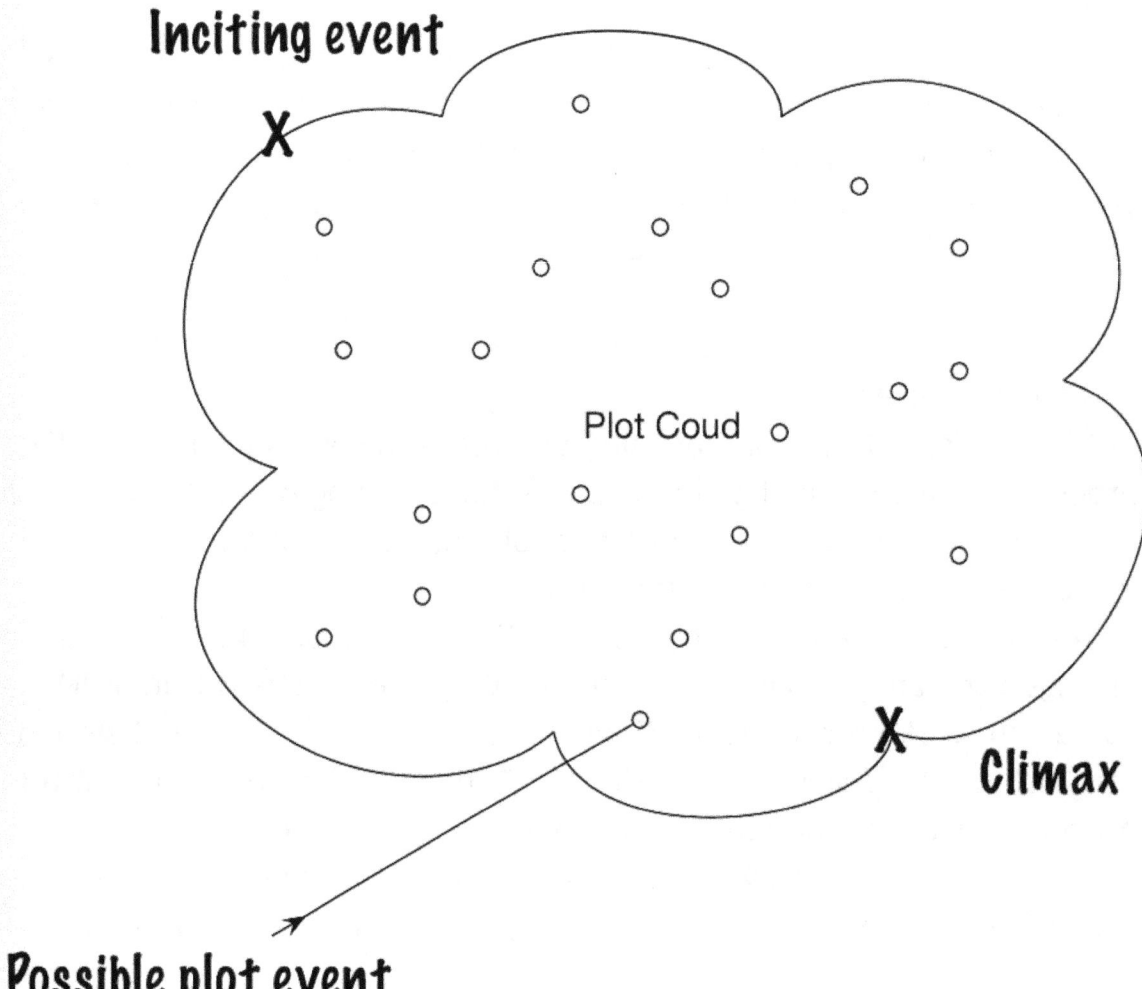

There are an infinite number of possible plot events in the plot cloud.
That means there are an infinite number of plot paths that connect the beginning and end points.

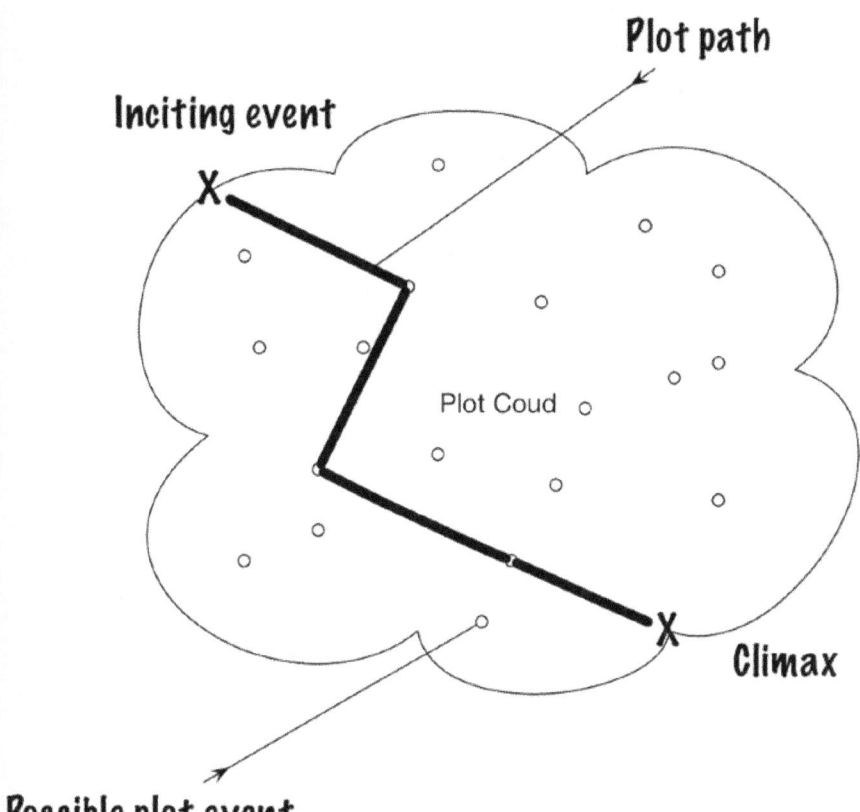

To connect the inciting event and the climax, you need three plot points.

Plot Development
This graphic depicts the purpose of the plot in your story.

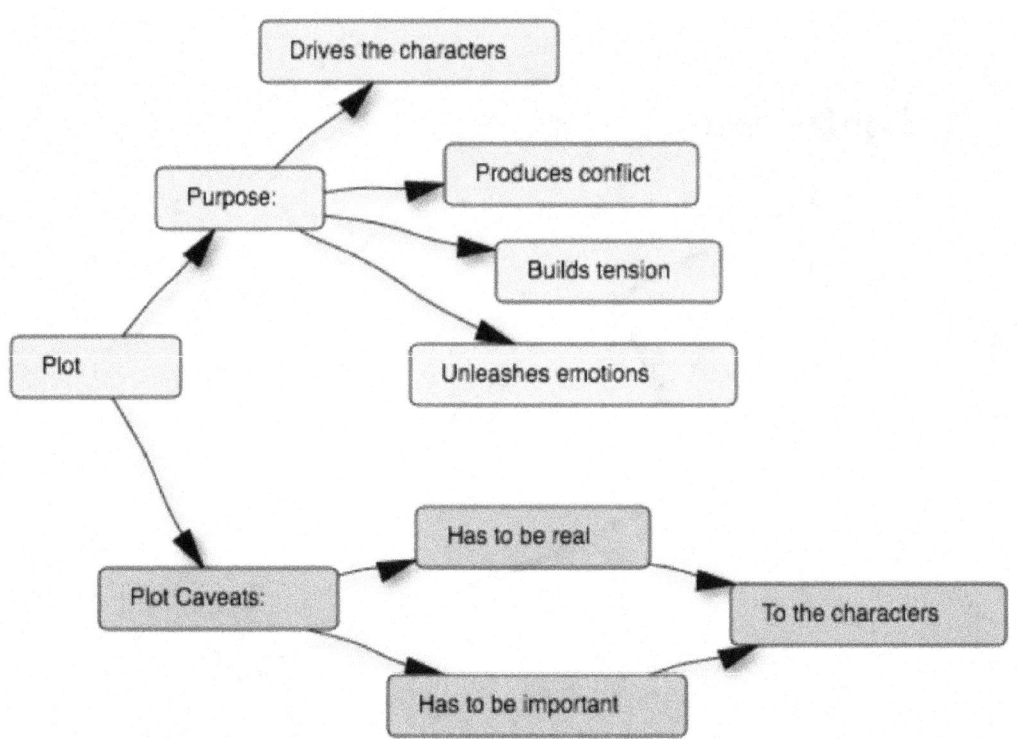

And the author has to convince the reader that the plot is real and important to the characters.

Constructing a plot

To repeat, a plot consists of a series of events that connect the inciting incident to the story's climax.

Events are not the same as incidents in this context. What's the difference? Events are major happenings or plot twists. Incidents are everyday occurrences. Humdrum and ordinary, they are the stuff that should be omitted from the story for the most part. For instance, let's suppose a character wakes up in the morning. If you then describe her routine of taking a shower, putting on makeup, selecting an outfit to wear to work and eating breakfast, these are all incidents. You, the author, have to ask yourself why am I even writing about this stuff? All it does is slow down the story, consume words and bore the readers.

However, if the woman's estranged husband replaced the water in the water heater with sulphuric acid, then the shower becomes an event: a very messy one.

Constructing a plot is a three-step process. The first step is to come up with a plot problem for the characters to work on. The second step is to develop the story's ending. The third step is to develop a series of events to connect step one and step two. After that, you are ready to write the first draft, provided all the other design work has been completed.

That's all there is to it, but don't be deceived by this simple formula. It's hard work.

Generic plot path

Let's develop a generic plot path for a story.

Step one: Hero recognizes the plot problem. (inciting event)
Step two: Hero makes an effort to solve the plot problem and fails.
Step three: A second and more serious effort also fails.
Step four: A third desperate attempt ends in a disaster.
Step five: A do-or-die attempt follows.
Step six: The hero succeeds (or not). (validation scene)

In a short story, these steps could become the scenes in the story. In a longer work, each step can be one or more chapters.

Successive failures

Why all the failures?

To jerk the reader around emotionally.

As the protagonist repeatedly fails, the tension increases and the characters' emotions become stronger.

The tension and the emotions affect the readers and keep them turning the pages.

Conflict

One of the main purposes of a plot is to generate conflict within the cast of characters. While the conflict can be between two characters, a three-sided battle provides more opportunities for conflicts. This three-sided combat also leads to the concept of a conflict triangle. Each of the three characters is now striving against two opponents. Character A and Character B can represent the protagonist and antagonist. Character C can be a sidekick or even a third main character who tries to outwit both A and B.

This is a very powerful technique to increase the conflict and the resultant tension in a story. Over the course of the story, the architecture of the triangle can change. An example of this can happen if Character B becomes an ally of Character A against Character C.

Assignment 5

In this assignment, take a story idea and use it to develop the story's plot.

Start with the plot problem.

Then get an ending.

Next, come up with the events linking the inciting event and the climax.

Once you've done all that, ask yourself: Do I really believe in this plot path? Can I really write a story using this plot path.

Lesson 6: Subplots

Subplot uses
Subplots have a number of uses. Here is a list of the main ones.
- Distract the reader from the main conflict.
- Give the reader a break from the main story.
- Stretch out the tension.
- Build the anticipation.
- Explore and develop other characters.
- Provide foreshadowing.

Let's explore each use.

Distracting the reader is a device that can be used in many stories. While the reader is engrossed in the subplot, the sneaky main characters are off doing something that will surprise the reader when she finds out what they did.

Give the reader a break: If the plot is especially intense, the readers will appreciate a break. The subplot gives them a chance to catch their breath and cool off a bit before they plunge back into the main plot.

Stretch out the tension: The subplots also make the main plot seem longer, stretching out the tension.

Build anticipation: This stretching out with subplots will build the anticipation of the reader to reach the climax.

Explore and develop other characters: The subplots can be used to explore less important characters and give the readers insights into these characters.

Provide foreshadowing: A subplot can be used to show a development that seemingly is independent of the main plot but is actually a crucial element in the climactic scenes.

Subplot example
Here is an example of a simple subplot suitable for a short story. Jim is the protagonist in the story and Harry is Jim's sidekick After the story gets

going and the reader is acquainted with both men, Jim says, "Harry, what's up? You look like something is bothering you."

"It's my mother, Jim. She had a heart attack last night and she's in intensive care."

A scene or two later.

"How's your mother doing?" Jim asked.

"Gonna have open heart surgery this afternoon," Harry replied.

"Oh, man. I hope she comes through all right."

Another scene or two passes.

"Is your mother okay?" Jim asked.

"She's great." Harry grinned at his friend. "The operation was a success. She'll be home within a week."

Harry and his mother's problem is a full subplot even though we never meet the mother. It characterizes Harry by showing his concern for her health. It characterizes Jim by demonstrating his sympathy for Harry's situation.

More subplot stuff

Subplots shouldn't stop the main plot from going forward. By this I mean, don't insert an entire five-thousand-word subplot in between two main plot scenes. The subplot scenes should be spaced out and interwoven with the main plot and other subplots. A complicated subplot can run for the entire length of the main plot or a simpler subplot can wrap up during a single part of the story.

The subplots can involve less important characters or they can involve the main characters. In this latter case, the protagonist will have two or even three problems to work on. This can lead to overload for the character and greatly increase the tension and his emotional upheaval.

Subplots must be handled in a way that interweaves them with the main plot. In many cases, the subplot will impact on the main plot's development and either hinder or help that development.

Nesting

Subplots have a structure; they can't just be thrown into the story any which way the author wants. If you have more than one subplot you have to categorize them from most important to least important. The subplots are then nested within the main story line. This nesting arrangement is depicted in the diagram with Subplot A as the most important and Subplot C as the least important.

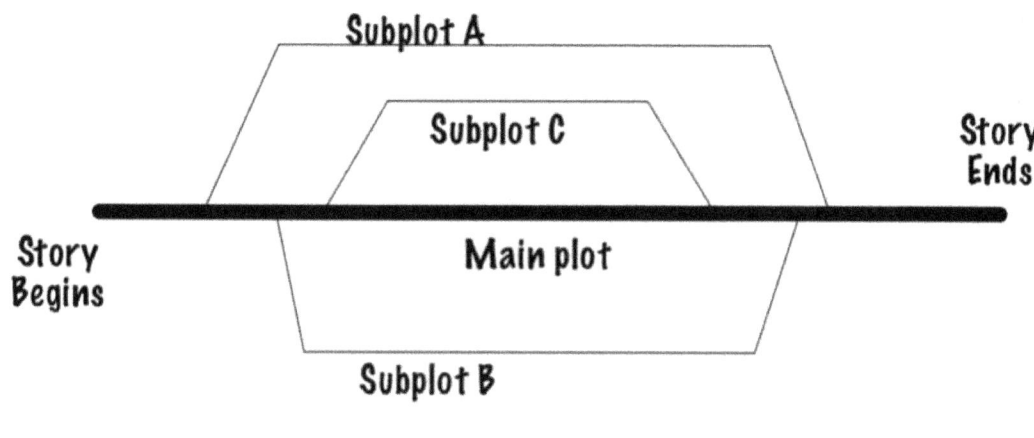

Nesting Subplots

Here is a description on how the nesting would be implemented in the above diagram.

In the diagram, the heavy black line represents story time, i.e., time within the story as experienced by the characters. This line also represents the main plot.

After the characters are introduced and the plot problem recognized, a scene from Subplot A can be added. After a number of scenes from the main plot and an occasional one from Subplot A, Subplot B is introduced. More Main plot scenes are broken up by scenes from Subplots A and B. Then Subplot C is begun. Now the bulk of the story continues with the subplot scenes dropped in to break up the Main plot.

When the story approaches the climax, Subplot C is finished first. The Main plot continues and Subplot B is closed out. The Main plot moves closer to the climax and Subplot A is finished up. Now the way is clear for the reader (and the author) to concentrate on the story's climax.

It is not good form to have a subplot continue beyond the climactic scene from the main storyline. Once the climax is reached and the validation scene shown, the story is over. The validation scene sums up the hero's journey and tells the reader what the hero gained for all his efforts. This could be; the love of a woman, financial independence, proving his innocence.

After this, the reader will no longer be interested in the outcome of a subplot. This means the validation scene is the end of the story. Don't keep adding scenes.

Assignment 6

Come up with an idea for at least one subplot in your story. Write a brief storyline for each subplot you wish to use.

Lesson 7: Scene design

Scene design

Scenes are how your story is created

I often see social media posts from a writer who claims she wrote 1500 words today. Or 5231. Or 219. That's fine when writing articles or papers but not for a story. When I'm working on a new story, I don't care how many words I wrote that day because I write scenes. I write one scene a day and I don't care how many words it is.

Scenes are the building blocks of a story. Not words, not sentences, not paragraphs, not chapters. Scenes.

Scenes have to be designed and they have mandatory requirements: a scene goal and an emotional arc.

Scenes need a structure to keep them from rambling on and on *ad infinitum*. The scene should be restricted to a specific time. The scene should be restricted to a specific location. For example, if a scene takes place in a schoolyard basketball court, a different scene should be developed to continue the action that night in a tavern. Similarly, if a scene involves Jim, who is in Manhattan, a second scene will be required to involve Sam, who is in Denver.

The scene must accomplish one of several purposes. It must characterize someone or pass vital information to the reader or it must move the story closer to the climax. If the scene accomplishes none of these, it should be deleted since all it does is add to the word count without accomplishing anything useful.

Optional requirements

Let's talk about optional requirements first.

Previously, I discussed the importance of giving readers the information to allow them to build images. Sensory information and scene setting are the tools to do that.

Sensory information is good to have but isn't absolutely necessary. This refers to touch, taste, smell, hearing. Sight is always included since that is how the point of view character is describing things.

The scene setting is a subset of the story setting. If the setting of your story is the Sahara Desert, then scenes can be set on a sand dune, at an oasis, in a sand storm, at a deserted fort.

The important issue here is that you give the reader the words necessary to build an image of the scene setting.

Usually, the writer uses omniscient POV to describe the setting and then switches to a character's POV.

Besides the location, the setting details can include the weather and the season, the time of day (or night) and any other pertinent information.

It's helpful here to make a sketch of the area in the scene. This is especially useful if the setting will be used in multiple scenes.

Scene goal

The purpose of a story is to take the reader on a journey. That journey is made up of scenes.

In a short story, the scene goal is usually related to solving the plot problem. In a novel, the scene goal can be related to a number of objectives.

Typical examples of scene goals are: to get vital information, to reach a specific location, to identify someone. These goals are waypoints in the movement of the story. Some scene goals may be accomplished within a single scene, or the goal may require several scenes before it is reached or completed. For instance, to reach a specific location can take many scenes, each one moving the characters closer to the location.

A short story may have six to ten or twelve scenes, while an average-sized novel may demand one-hundred-fifty or more scenes.

To repeat, the basic requirement for these scenes is that it characterizes someone or passes on relevant information or moves the reader closer to the journey's end: the story's climax.

Characterizing scenes: talk about a character's background or mental makeup or internal monologue.

Relevant information: can be a clue, a murderer's name, a secret location, a spell.

Assignment 7

Time to outline the scenes in your story.

I block out ten to twelve scenes at a time. For each scene, I write a one or two sentence synopsis, list the characters in the scene and where it takes place.

Use your story idea and the plot to block out the scenes in the story. Or block out the scenes in the opening chapter of a longer story.

Lesson 8: Emotional arc

Emotional arc

Readers want to experience and share the characters' emotional journey. In order to create this emotional journey, each scene must have an emotional change in it. What this means is that the character's emotion at the end of the scene must be changed from the character's emotion at the start of the scene. Whether the change is positive or negative is irrelevant. A scene with a flat emotional arc is not a good scene.

An additional requirement is that the character's emotional change in a scene must be linked to the ending emotion in the previous scene and become the beginning emotion in the succeeding scene. In other words, the emotional changes form a continuous arc that stretches from the story's opening scene to the climatic scene at the end. Stories with multiple main characters will have multiple emotional arcs, one for each main character.

Example

A simple example of this is illustrated here.

In this scenario, the starting emotion for Scene Y is the same as the ending emotion in Scene X. And Scene Z picks up where Scene Y left off. This example is for a single character.

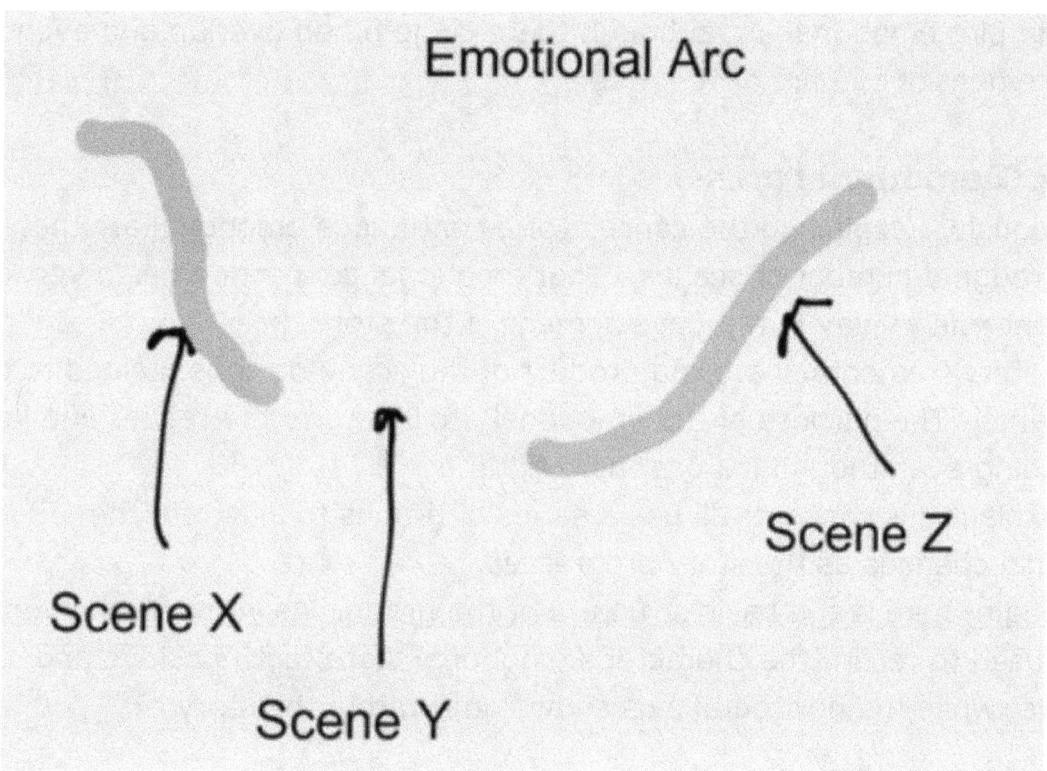

With multiple main characters and emotional arcs, this continuous arc would be interrupted by the scenes from the other emotional arcs. Thus, keeping track of each character's emotional arc is yet another chore for the author.

For a short story, developing this arc is relatively simple because of the small number of scenes involved. The situation is more complicated in a long story because of the many scenes involved and the multiple points of view and subplots.

More on emotional arcs

Let's simplify this mind-boggling concept. The emotional arc I'll describe belongs to a single character, not the entire cast. However, each major character needs his own emotional arc. Yeah, that's right. Both the antagonist and the protagonist need an emotional arc. The sidekicks can and should have one also, especially if they star in their own subplots.

Further, the main characters can have more than one emotional arc. For instance, the hero can have an emotional arc for the main plot and another emotional arc for a subplot. The subplot emotional arc will be different from the main plot emotional arc although there could be an overlap and even reinforcement of one arc or the other.

Plot & emotional arcs-1

Previously, I explained the concept of a continuous emotional arc that runs through a number of scenes. That emotional connection has a very important role to play in the development of the story.

The story's emotional arc is a product of the scene designs melded to the plot events. The purpose of the emotional arc is to grip the reader and keep her reading even though it's past her bedtime.

To explain this concept, I'll use a series of graphs to illustrate the emotional changes as the story progresses.

To begin, here is the basic structure of the graph. As you see, the vertical axis is used to record the character's emotional state, both positive and negative, while the horizontal axis shows time within the story.

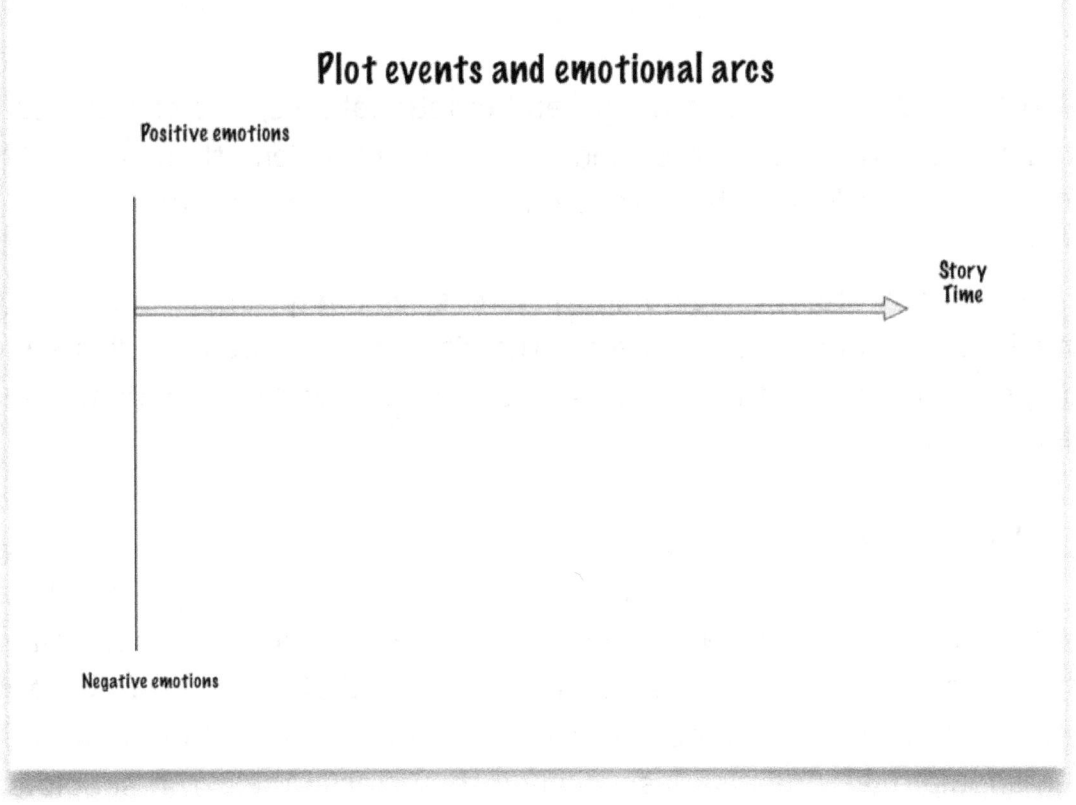

Plot & emotional arcs-2

We can now construct an emotional curve as your story unfolds. I'll explain this one step at a time. The story begins with the protagonist in a positive emotional state. Life is good, he's cool, everything is grand.

Plot events and emotional arcs

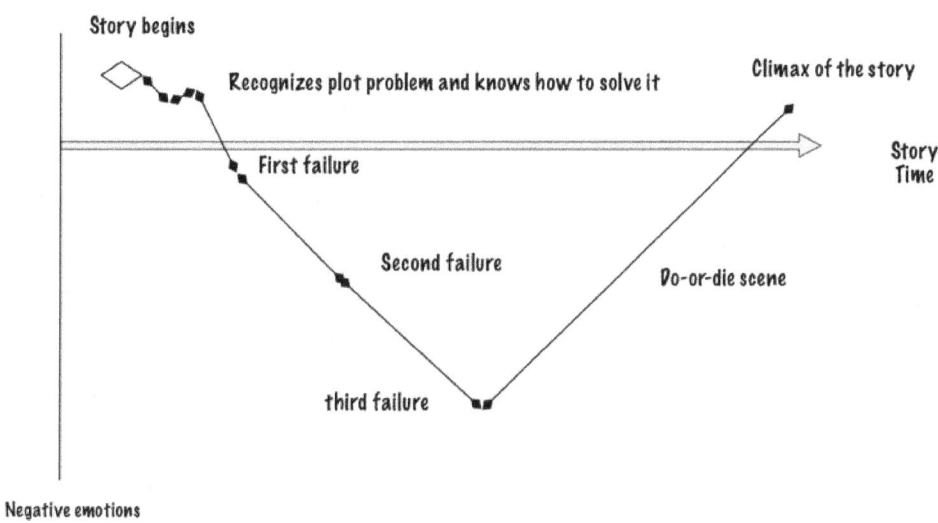

Then he recognizes the plot problem and his emotional state drops a bit lower. He's not quite as happy as he was. "Why me?" he moans. "I don't have time for this stuff." But then he thinks of a way to solve the problem and his emotional state improves. He puts his plan into action and it fails. "Uh-oh, this isn't as easy as I thought it would be." This failure results in a drop in his emotional state.

He ponders the situation and comes up with another plan.

His second attempt also fails and now he's getting alarmed. His emotional state plunges deeper into negative territory.

These attempts can be a single scene or they can involve a number of scenes, but each scene has to result in a lowering of the emotional state. Struggling on, he develops still another plan and executes it.

Again he fails and his emotional state has now sunk into depression. After wallowing around for a while, he sucks it up and decides he'll solve the problem or die trying. At this point, your story has reached the beginning of the climax.

Plot & emotional arcs-3

As the hero struggles through the climactic scene, his emotional state soars (or not, if he doesn't succeed, which is always an option).

Don't forget, the climactic scene must be followed by the validation scene.

The chart depicts the hero's emotional journey. The bad guy also has an emotional journey and it's the exact opposite of the good guy's journey. Every time the protagonist fails, the antagonist wins and his emotional state shoots up while the protagonist's falls.

This overall process of constructing an emotional arc is how a compelling story is put together. Whether you draw a chart, use an outline or a mind-map, you have to track these emotional changes in order to properly develop the story's emotional arc. It won't do to have the protagonist's emotional arc bounce around and go positive before the story's ending. The protagonist's emotions can improve and tick upward (slightly) but this has to be a temporary situation, and his downward spiral must continue soon afterward.

For a short story, each of the failures can be a scene. In a longer work, each failure can be one or more chapters long or even an entire act.

Assignment 8

Develop a preliminary version of the emotional arc for your protagonist. How will her emotions change during the story as a result of plot events? The actual emotions used as you write the story will probably change. Expect that to happen. Don't lock into the preliminary emotions. Be flexible.

Lesson 9: Point of view

Point of view

In this lesson, I'll concentrate on point of view. POV is the most technical aspect of story writing, and mastering it requires practice. It's very easy to screw this up and confuse the reader. POV comes down to this: who is telling the story: the author, the characters or both. You should minimize the author's involvement.

I'll discuss three types of POV: omniscient, third person limited and first person.

Deciding on a point of view, who the POV character is, and whether or not there will be multiple POV characters are important decisions an author has to make before starting to write the first draft. A first person story is quite different from a third person story, and the difference isn't just in the pronouns used.

First person POV stories are highly restrictive in what the author can do and not do. Third person POV stories offer more flexibility and fewer limitations.

As an example of the choices facing an author, consider these third person point of view options.

Your primary POV character can be the protagonist. This is the choice in many stories. An alternative is to use the antagonist as the primary POV character. In this case the story is told from the perspective of the bad guy, not the good guy. A third alternative is to use the protagonist's sidekick as the main POV character. The sidekick character now serves primarily as a narrator or a reporter, telling the reader what the protagonist is doing and how he is reacting to situations. If you take a single story and consider the implications of writing it from each of these three different POV characters, you will see that each instance will produce a story that is quite different from the other two.

Omniscient POV

In this POV the author has god-like knowledge. She knows everything, sees everything and even knows the future of the characters. You know what each character is thinking, what their moods are and what they plan to do.

This POV was used to used to write entire novels once. Think Dickens and Moby Dick. Now it s used primarily to introduce scenes and describe the location. Then the author switches to another POV.

This POV is depicted in the graphic.

Third person limited POV

In this point of view, the narrator is a character rather than the author. The scenes are related through the eyes and ears of a character. This POV character does NOT know what the other characters are thinking or what they are about to do. The POV character can guess the others' emotional state by observing their speech and body language, but this POV character does not know what is going on in their minds. That is the main difference between this viewpoint and the omniscient viewpoint.

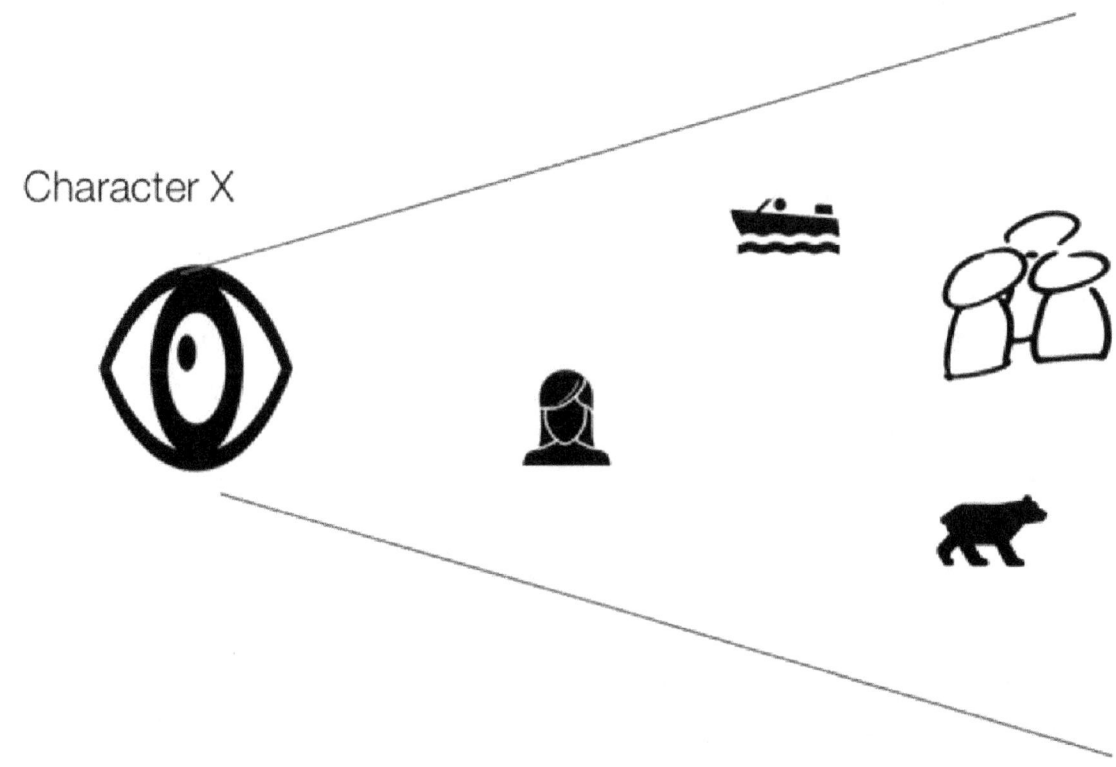

The secret to writing in this POV is for the author to get inside the POV character's mind and write the scene from there. Believe me, this is strange the first few times you try it, but after a while, it becomes quite natural. Of course, this POV scheme is restrictive. Unlike omniscient POV, this POV character can't know what is happening in the building across the street. In the beginning, there is a tendency for the inexperienced writer to break out of the POV character's mind to tell the reader stuff the POV character can't possibly know. Often, this will entail telling the reader what a different character is thinking or about to do.

Trust me, readers may not understand the technical details of POV restrictions, but they know when it's done incorrectly.

First person POV

In first person POV, the narrator and the POV character are one and the same. The entire story is told from inside the mind of this POV character. The reader can see, hear and learn only what that POV character can see, hear and learn. For this reason the author has to get deep inside the head of this character and has to become quite intimate with the character.

The graphic for first person POV is the same as for third person limited POV.

POV examples

Here are examples on how each type of POV looks to the reader.

Omniscient: *The old forest was gloomy and humid. Not even a hint of a breeze stirred the leaves. Occasionally a small shaft of sunlight broke through and illuminated a small patch of ground. Vines hung from the lower limbs of the huge oak trees and thick spider webs filled in the spaces between vines and limbs.*

In this case the narrator is the author telling the reader what the forest looks like.

Third person limited: *Jack traveled through a gloomy forest. Already sweat soaked his shirt. Ahead, a small ray of sunshine somehow evaded the thick umbrella of oak limbs and shone on a pile of moldy leaves. Jack ducked under a vine hanging from a tree limb and sidestepped a thick spider web.*

Here we see the forest narrated by a character who uses actions and feelings to help the description: soaked shirt, ducking, sidestepping. This type of narrator brings the reader closer to the action than in the previous example.

First person: *I had a sense of foreboding about the gloomy forest. Even the small shaft of sunlight ahead didn't do anything to lighten my mood. Sweat ran down my nose and dripped on my already soaked shirt. I had to duck under a drooping vine to move ahead and edge around a thick spider web.*

This time, the description is even more personal and the reader is brought even closer to the forest. That is the consequence of using a first person narrator.

Notice how different each scene appears to the reader.

Assignment 9

Decide what POV you'll use to write the story.
Decide which character will be the POV character.

Lesson 10: Story-telling techniques

In this lesson I won't talk about story design. Rather I'll discuss how you hold the reader's attention and keep her turning the pages.

Verb tense

One of the initial decisions an author must make is what verb tense to use in the story. Most nonfiction utilizes the present tense as does this book. Most fiction uses the past tense, although a number of fiction books now use the present tense. In all my novels I use the past tense. It just feels like the correct way to tell the story. Reading a present tense novel doesn't seem right to me. It's like there is something that needs to be fixed or redone.

In telling a story, there are other tenses that could be used, such as the future tense. This could be a time traveler relating what will happen in the future. I think stories that use unusual tenses will initially surprise and intrigue a reader, but they will quickly lose their luster and end up turning the reader off.

I recommend using the past tense. The past tense is so common it's almost invisible to the reader. This invisibility makes it easy for the reader to slip comfortably into the story and will in no way interfere with the readers' enjoyment.

Stimulus and reaction

Stimuli and reactions are the basic couplet of actions in a story. It is cause and effect done small. It's a simple principle and easy to understand, yet the couplet is often done incorrectly and this leads to confusion for the reader.

The correct sequence for the couplet is 1) a stimulus occurs and 2) a reaction follows. Despite the simplicity of this formula, the components are often reversed or even worse, one of the components is omitted.

What is a stimulus? It can be a punch, a kiss, a dirty look or a pistol shot, to give a few examples. It's a "happening."

What is a reaction? It can be a defensive move, a sense of surprise, returning a dirty look or diving behind a barrel.

I often see examples in which the reaction occurs before the stimulus. Even worse, the writer describes a character's reaction but omits the stimulus. I'll bet you've read stories in which a character reacts and you stop reading because you know you missed something. Rereading a few paragraphs doesn't fill in the blank space. The problem is the author omitted the stimulus and left you trying to figure out why the reaction occurred.

A popular version of this broken couplet is, "Character A smiled/grinned/growled, etc." In these cases, the author doesn't bother telling us why Character A did what he did.

Let's examine this basic concept in more detail using examples.

Jody panicked. This is a reaction minus a stimulus.

Jody panicked. A dead body lay on the floor. This is better, but the reaction precedes the stimulus.

John dived behind a barrel. A shot rang out. Here the reaction occurs before the stimulus.

Sally threw a drink in Alex's face. This is a reaction, but no stimulus is shown, unless the stimulus occurred in preceding sentences or scenes and this is a delayed reaction.

Foreshadowing

Foreshadowing is a useful device in which the author plants clues or hints.

There is an old stage play adage that goes like this: If you need a gun in the last scene, you'd better show the gun to the audience in the first scene. Audiences and readers don't like stories that have characters using stuff the author never told them about, like the gun above.

You can also use material from the character's biography to foreshadow important events later in the story. Recall this example I used previously: a character has a fear of open water such as a lake or the sea. This fear is based on an event when he was a five-year-old. Back then, the character almost drowned. At the climax of the story, the character is faced with a situation in which he has to save a person drowning in a lake. Does the character overcome his fear of water and save the person? Or does he walk away and hope no one saw him? Of course, to use this foreshadowing, the author has to show the character's fear of water early in the story and explain it.

Show don't tell

Many instructors and books on writing urge writers to "show" the story to the reader rather than "tell" it. This is absurd. The vast majority of every book is "telling." Showing certainly is something that an author should use, but its use has to be judicious. If a writer uses too much showing, the reader will get bored and stop reading.

There are many opportunities for "showing" in any story. The writer has to understand how to use them and how to spot opportunities. Showing can be used to "show" the character's emotion or a bit of action.

Let's try a few more examples.

Sally nervously looked at her watch.

In this example, the author directly tells the reader what Sally's emotional state is.

Sally shredded a paper napkin, fidgeted on her chair and glanced at her watch.

In this case, the author doesn't tell the reader what Sally's emotional state is. Instead the author depicts a woman acting nervously. It's up to the reader to decipher the words to determine Sally's emotional state. And readers love to do this.

Here's another example.

Margo reacted angrily.

As before, the author tells the reader about the character's mental state

Margo scowled, placed her hands on her hips and stamped her foot.

Here, the reader has to interpret the author's words to understand what is happening.

He entered the room hesitantly.

The use of an adverb is often an indication of an action that can be converted to showing. The sentence above can be rewritten to show a guy walking hesitantly.

"Help me," she said imploringly.

A dialog tag and an adverb is always telling and should be replaced with showing. Here you should show the woman sobbing and pleading as she says, "Help me."

Dialog and exposition

An author can pass information to the reader in one of two ways. The author can have characters discuss or argue about a situation and, in the course of the dialog, insert the information. Internal monologue is the second way. In this situation, the author chooses to tell the reader about it using exposition.

In the reader's viewpoint, dialog is more interesting than internal monologue and exposition. In most cases, the dialog choice will require more words.

Of course, if the author needs to enter a character's mind and engage in internal monologue, this has to be exposition. An exception could be made if the character suffers from multiple personalities. In this case, the different personalities could hold an internal conversation to discuss a situation.

While exposition is necessary, it should be limited whenever it can. This is especially true when it comes to info dumps. Info dumps are those deadly, dense passages filled with information the author thinks the reader has to know. Perhaps the reader does need to know this stuff, but an info dump ensures the material will not be read. It won't be read because many, many readers skip info dumps and flip through the pages until they come to a more interesting part.

See the section on world-building in the first chapter phase 1 for further discussion on info dumps.

One effective use for exposition is employed at the beginning of scenes to describe the scene setting.

Assignment 10

Look over material you've already written.

1 Find examples where the stimulus/reaction couplets are done incorrectly

2 Find instances where you can rewrite telling to showing.

Lesson 11: Dialog

Who is telling the story?

Stories can be told by the author or the characters. If it's the author, the story will be told through exposition. If it's the characters, the story will be told through dialog.

Readers prefer to hear from the characters, so authors should butt out and let the character tell the story.

Formatting

Dialog has formatting requirements. Readers are accustomed to seeing the dialog correctly formatted. If these rules are violated, it will jerk the reader out of the story.

Basic dialog:

"Blah blah blah," Jane said.

Note the punctuation in the example.

Continuing dialog:

"Blah blah blah," Jane said. "Yadda yadda yadda."

When switching characters, always start a new paragraph for the new dialog.

Must be realistic

Dialog must sound like real people speaking. It can't be stilted nor use artificial phrasing. A truck driver can't talk like a college professor. A bank manager can't talk like a street punk.

A good way to test dialog is to record it using your cell phone, than play it back and listen. Does it sound like people you talk to all the time? No? Rewrite it.

Dialog, not conversation

Dialog must move the story forward or characterize someone. If the dialog doesn't do one of these two things, then the dialog is really conversation.

What's the difference? Dialog moves the story forward; conversation stops it in its tracks. Rewrite or delete the conversation

Realistic talking

When people speak, they use 'was' and 'were' in almost every sentence. The use 'wanna, gonna, gotta'. They drop the g from words ending in -ing.

For your dialog to be realistic, it must use these conventions. Otherwise, it will appear stilted and unnatural. In other words, dialog must use speaking voices,, not writing voices.

Assignment 11

As you write the first draft, stop after each scene is completed and review the dialog in that scene. Recording it is a great way to review dialog.

Is it dialog or conversation?

Is it stilted or natural sounding?

How does it sound when recorded?

Revise as necessary.

Lesson 12: Assorted topics

Central metaphor

A central metaphor will change an ordinary story into something special. It is a recurring image that a character uses throughout the story. However, it is not easy to build a new one for each story. Sometimes I can't come up with one no matter how hard I try. Sometimes the only one I can think of is one I've already used, and I don't want to repeat the central metaphor in another novel.

Example-1

A low-ranking alien officer struggles to get ahead on her ability in a military society that views assassination and treachery as the preferred method of advancement. She pictures herself as a ship of sanity sailing on a sea of madness searching for a safe harbor. Later on, when she faces difficulties, she imagines her ship careening toward a rocky shore. After another setback, she sees her unarmed ship of sanity being pursued by a pirate fleet. This is the central metaphor from my novel *Zaftan Miscreants*.

Example-2

A young roaming bailiff sets out on his first law-enforcement mission and imagines himself to be an eagle leaving the nest for its initial flight. After a screwup, he wonders if young eagles make mistakes. After a second botched assignment, he asks himself how a young eagle would go about covering its tracks. This is from a novella called *Chasing Dreams*.

But . . .

A few references to the character's image will have the reader buying-in to the metaphor. Just don't overdo it by bringing up the central metaphor in every scene.

Crisis management

Let's say that in the course of a scene your character runs into a terrifying situation. Getting the character into these situations is easy. Getting him out is not so easy and you also have to deal with the emotional trauma involved. You can show the character getting away from whatever is so terrifying, perhaps by backing out of the immediate area, but you still can't ignore the strong emotion the character experienced. Your character has gone through a terrifying emotional change; you have to show that emotion getting dissipated.

Crisis management example

I'll use an event in a recent short story of mine as an example. The character Leofric runs into a squad of hostile archers:

"Stand or die," a snarling voice said from Leofric's left. He turned and faced a notched arrow pointing at his head. A surge of fear spread upward from Leofric's groin. Six other archers emerged from the trees. Each wore a forest green jerkin and hose. The one who spoke had a hood on his jerkin. Pulled forward, it hid his face in shadows. Leofric froze and almost stopped breathing. He wondered who the archers were and what they intended to do.

"Now then," the first archer said. "Let's begin the trial. Me name is Jackey and this is me patch of land. Trespass at your peril. Are you Norman scum?"

"I . . . never met a Norman," Leofric said. He turned his head slightly so he could see all the archers with his peripheral vision. He couldn't figure a way to get out of this mess without getting killed. At this short range, the arrows couldn't miss.

"You a Welsh raider?"

"No," Leofric replied.

"A murderer onna run?"

"No."

"A priest or a monk?" The archer slightly eased the tension on the bowstring and Leofric's fear lessened a notch.

"No."

"A lawyer?"

Leofric shook his head.

Jackey shifted his feet and sighed. Leofric thought he might get out of this situation alive.

"Well, if you ain't any of them things, you can use me forest." Jackey pointed the arrow at the ground.

Leofric gulped air and let his taut muscles relax.

As you can see, I showed Leofric's great fear evaporating as the archer became less hostile. In other words, I defused Leofric's crisis. If I didn't, the reader would be left wondering what happened to the great fear Leofric experienced and how he got out of it.

Adverbs

Adverbs are a component of our speaking habits, and they are one of my pet peeves. I really hate them. So does Stephen King, who once said (or wrote), "T*he road to Hell is paved with adverbs*." I actually have an adverb budget. I allocate two or, at the most, three adverbs per five thousand words.

However, I have to admit that my first drafts are studded with adverbs. There is a good reason for this. When writing a first draft, my objective is to get the story down on paper as fast as possible. Adverbs are great for this purpose because they are easy to use and allow me to write faster. During the second and third draft, I remove as many adverbs as I possibly can. To do this requires some creativity and heavy thinking. By the time I finish a third or fourth draft, you'd be hard pressed to find an adverb in the story.

Empty words

Here is a partial list of empty words we use when speaking: *very, even, ever, really, still, just, then*. I'm sure you can come up with many more. And there's "*like*" used as a comma or in place of a pause. Don't use these in your writing.

However, sometimes these words aren't empty. On occasion they actually add meaning to a sentence. How can you tell?

Use the Empty Word Test:

Step 1) Remove the word from the sentence.

Step 2) Did the meaning of the sentence change?

Step 3a) If yes, it's not an empty word. Keep it

Step 3b) If no, it's an empty word. Remove it.

Assignment 12:

Develop a central metaphor for your story without using adverbs or empty words.

Lesson 13: Wrapping it all up

Let's talk about something different
I'm done talking about story design and story telling. Now let's talk about actually getting the story out of your notes and onto paper.

Putting it all together
By now, you may have noticed that creating a story is a complicated operation. What with the characters, plots, setting, scenes and other stuff, new writers sometimes get paralyzed by wondering where to start.

I've bounced around a lot during these sessions. The way I introduced the topics isn't how I go about working up my stories. I'm going to show you how I do it. Maybe my way will work for you. Maybe not. Maybe you can modify what I do and develop your own way. I have a mind-map on how I do this stuff. It takes 9 steps. Look over the diagram. Once you understand how I do it, figure out a way that will work for you.

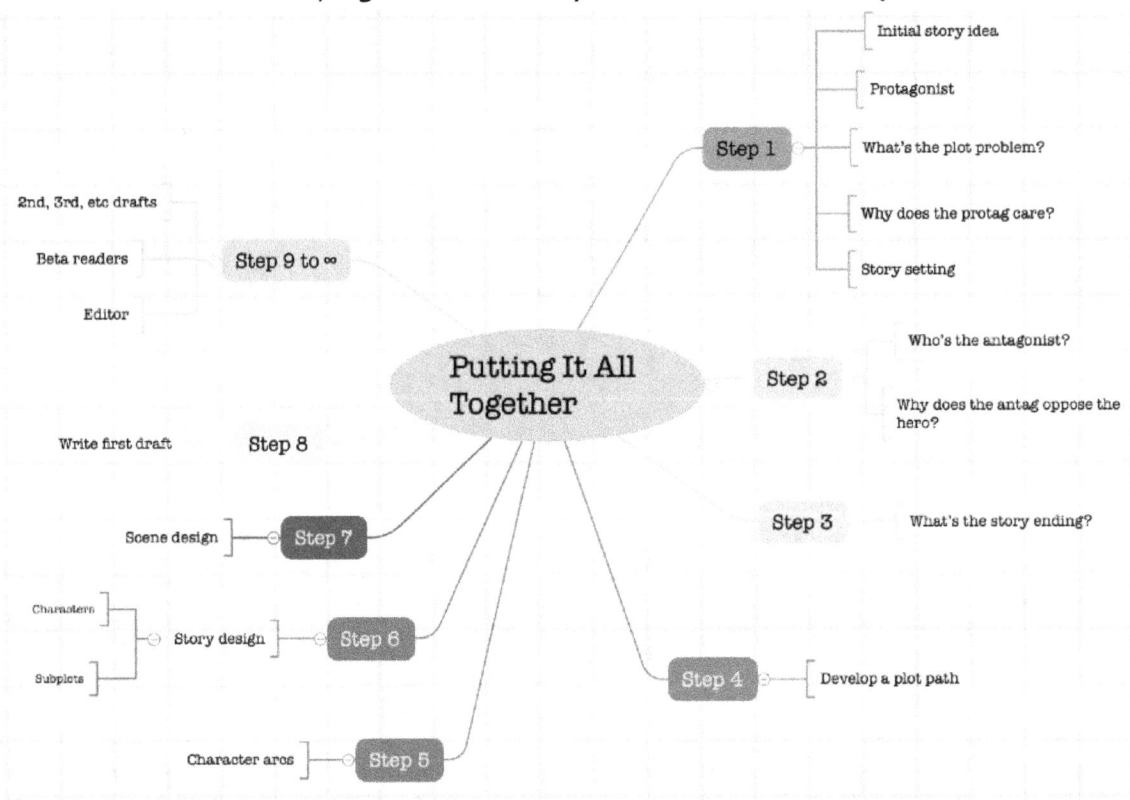

Writing apps

Writing a short story in Word is possible. Writing a novel in Word leads to insanity. You'll end up with hundreds of small files with obscure names.

I write all my books in a program called Scrivener. With it, each story has a single file. That file contains everything relating to the story: scenes, chapters, character sheets, notes, research, everything.

While you're writing and can't remember a detail about a character, that information is two clicks away with Scrivener. With Word, it could be an hour-long search for the proper file.

https://www.literatureandlatte.com/scrivener/overview

Miscellaneous stuff

First drafts

Ernest Hemingway, a Pulitzer-winning author, once said, "The first draft of anything is a piece of shit." My first drafts are and so will yours. No one sees my stuff until at least the third draft.

Beta readers (critiquers)

Once you've finished revising, you need other writers to look over the story and tell you where you screwed up. Writers not family members. You have to find writing groups or develop a list of writers you can work with.

Assignment 13

Write the first draft of your story.

Author Business

Table of Contents
Business startup. 65
Payments. 71
Keeping track. 75
Taxes. 80
Breaking even. 82
Start a publishing company? 85
Resources. 88

Starting a business

Here is something to think about. If you are a published author, you have a business waiting to blossom. The question is when you'll start doing it. Most newbie authors recognize the need for a business only after the book is published and they are wrestling with marketing issues or taxes.

A more appropriate time to begin the business is before the manuscript is completely finished. This gives an author time to properly plan the startup business and think about the decisions that have to be made. Ideally, you can do this when the manuscript is 'finished' and packed off to an editor. An editor will take a month or more and you'll have little to do on the book during that time. So why not get started on developing your author business?

Yeah, I know you really don't need another bunch of tasks to work on, but this is important. Your success as an author may depend on this work.

No matter when you decide to start the business, this chapter will be relevant.

It's not the same situation if you write and sell short stories, essays, articles or poems. In these cases, the market that bought the item will pay a set fee for the right to publish your piece. Your compensation in this case doesn't change whether the market sells a hundred or a thousand copies of the magazine. With book publication, the author's compensation (royalties) depends entirely on book sales. No book sales, no royalties.

In the process of selling the books, you will incur expenses. These could be marketing costs or they could be expenses incurred with self-publishing the book.

You'll need money to pay these expenses. Where does it come from? Preferably, it comes from royalties or possibly from a loan. Or you could fund the money from your personal accounts. If the money earned exceeds these expenses, you and your company will show a profit and you can pay back the loan. See, it's simple.

Think like a CEO

I believe a major reason that authors fail to sell books is because they don't think like a business owner. Businesses use highly developed marketing plans to introduce a new product to the public. These businesses do that because it has been proven to work.

Many inexperienced authors use a shotgun approach to marketing (when they do *any* marketing!). Their efforts are without a focus and are piecemeal instead of continuous. In other words, the marketing proceeds without a plan to direct those activities. Most often, the author-business also, will be without a plan.

A business plan will focus the energies of the company (you!) on the important aspects. A marketing plan organizes your efforts to tell the world about the book.

You are the Chief Executive Officer or CEO of the author-business and you are also the Marketing Manager for the book. Since you are also responsible for the budget and tracking revenue, you are the Chief Financial Officer or CFO. Because you are the author, you get to create all the copy required by the marketing manager.

A business needs an organization chart so everyone in the company can see where they stand in the hierarchy. Here is the organization chart for your company.

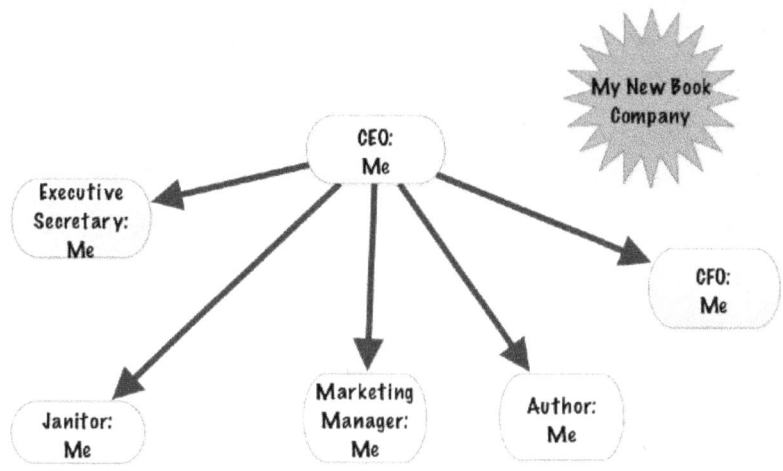

By the way, I should point out that none of these jobs pays very well.

What type of business?

There are two different types of business you can start. One is called a Sole Proprietorship and the other is known as a Limited Liability Corporation. Which one you choose is a personal decision. I chose the sole proprietorship when I started my author business. If I had it to do over again, I'd choose the LLC option. I think it would be more appropriate for the business I now run. In the beginning, the sole proprietorship suited my needs.

Sole proprietorship

From the SBA.gov website: https://www.sba.gov

"A sole proprietorship is easy to form and gives you complete control of your business. You're automatically considered to be a sole proprietorship if you do business activities but don't register as any other kind of business.

Sole proprietorships do not produce a separate business entity. This means your business assets and liabilities are not separate from your personal assets and liabilities. You can be held personally liable for the debts and obligations of the business. Sole proprietors are still able to get a trade name. It can be hard to raise money because you can't sell stock, and banks are hesitant to lend to sole proprietorships.

Sole proprietorships can be a good choice for low-risk businesses and owners who want to test their business idea before forming a more formal business."

Limited liability corporation

From the SBA.gov website:

"An LLC lets you take advantage of the benefits of both the corporation and partnership business structures.

LLCs protect you from personal liability in most instances, your personal assets — like your vehicle, house, and savings accounts — won't be at risk in case your LLC faces bankruptcy or lawsuits.

Profits and losses can get passed through to your personal income without facing corporate taxes. However, members of an LLC are considered self-employed and must pay self-employment tax contributions towards Medicare and Social Security.

LLCs can have a limited life in many states. When a member joins or leaves an LLC, some states may require the LLC to be dissolved and re-formed with new membership — unless there's already an agreement in place within the LLC for buying, selling, and transferring ownership.

LLCs can be a good choice for medium- or higher-risk businesses, owners with significant personal assets they want protected, and owners who want to pay a lower tax rate than they would with a corporation."

Employer Identification Number (EIN)

Your company will need an EIN from the IRS (in the USA). In other countries there will be similar requirements and similar complications.

An Employer Identification Number (EIN) is also known as a federal tax identification number and is used to identify a business entity.

Since this is a federal government requirement, you'll have to fill out a form, send it in and wait quite a while to get your EIN.

Here is a link to instructions on how to get an EIN:

https://www.irs.gov/businesses/small-businesses-self-employed/employer-id-numbers

Resources

There is plenty of material available to assist you with your business planning. There is also a lot of "help" that is anything but. Like most things in life, be cautious of people or websites offering their "expertise" for only a "small" fee.

With the appearance of mobile devices, a number of apps focused on business planning have sprung up. I've found a few that are helpful and a few that are useless. The useless ones tend to be all of one kind and some of them are quite pricey. This class of apps consists of a series of questions on business planning followed by a text box where you type the answer. There is no explanation or discussion on why the question is asked or what its importance is. There is no discussion within the app to explain anything about a business plan. There are no insights into business planning. In other words, all these apps do is produce a written report consisting of nothing more than the questions and your answers.

It's difficult to tell how useful, or not, these apps are without buying them. My advice is to look at the reviews. If the app doesn't have any, don't spend money on it.

With that point out of the way, let's move on. https://www.capterra.com is a website that lists and compares software products for hundreds of categories, including business planning.

Browsing the Capterra site will give you a lot of options. The products listed are broken down by type of computer operating systems and by mobile devices.

Many software developers are moving to online applications rather than apps that can be downloaded to a computer or mobile device.

The Small Business Administration (SBA) is a federal government agency that has many programs that are useful to a small business (that's you). You can find it here: https://www.sba.gov

One of the features of the website is an online business planner. It will be well worth your time to establish an account and browse all the material available here, free of charge.

Payments

This is an important consideration. After all, you never know when you may sell some books and actually get royalty checks. So, you have to be prepared for that eventuality.

There are a number of ways that you can receive money from your book sales.

One way is directly from people who buy your book at events, appearances and lectures. You give them a book, preferably signed, and they hand you cash or a check. This is the simplest and most lucrative method since you don't have to split the revenue with a distributor or packager. However, reality says your appearances will most likely be geographically limited and so will these types of sales.

A second way to sell your book is via websites such as Draft2Digital, Amazon, Barnes & Noble and other sites. Unlike the personal selling mentioned above, you won't meet the buyer or even know who he or she is, so you won't be able to thank them for buying your book.

A third way to sell books is via bookstores and libraries. Similar to the web selling, you won't know who purchased your book.

Web selling and bookstore sales have one thing in common; when the book is sold, you don't get paid. You will eventually, but you'll have to wait a while. Several months in some cases. This is how the process works. Your packager or publisher distributes your books to the bookstores and websites. When your book is sold, the seller keeps part of the sales revenue and sends the remainder to the packager or publisher, who also keeps a portion. The remainder is your royalty

Before you can get your royalties, you'll have to set up channels to allow the publisher or packager to disburse the money to you. The options include a PayPal or similar site deposit or a direct deposit to a bank account. These two are known as Electronic Funds Transfer (EFT). Which option your packager wants you to use will be found somewhere on its website. They may limit your options. If you want a check mailed to your home, you're out of luck since publishers and packagers won't do it. They'll restrict your payments to some sort of EFT procedure.

Royalty splits: ebooks

Let's talk about what happens when books get sold through your packagers. You get some of the money and some of the money goes to the packagers and the distributors. How much does each get? Here is how four packagers split up the sales revenue. Let's assume your ebook sells for $3.99.

Draft2Digital: With this ebook packager, the revenue split is simple. If you sell an ebook through the D2D site, the split is 70/30 with you getting the 70% share. So for each ebook sold on the site, you get $2.80. If the book is sold through one of D2D's distributors, such as the IStore or B&N, the split is 60/40 and you make $2.40 on each book.

Kindle ebook: Here the ebook split becomes a bit more complicated because Kindle uses two revenue sharing plans. One plan calls for a 35/65 split and the other 70/30. The 70/30 split is not available if your book is priced at less than $2.99. If there are any advantages in keeping the 35/65 split for a book that is eligible for the 70/30 plan, I don't know what that advantage is. With your $3.99 book, you may not get exactly 70% because Kindle levies a delivery fee (???) on book sales. The fee depends upon the size of the file download. The bigger the file, the bigger the fee. If your book has a lot of graphics in it, the delivery fee can be large.

As with D2D, you'll get $2.80 for each book sold at the US Amazon site with the 70% split (less the delivery fee). Kindle doesn't use ebook distributors the way D2D does. Kindle won't place your book with other web sellers such as the Sony or Kobo sites, but it will put the book on non-USA Amazon sites. This is an option you have to select. Some of these sites have only the 35% option available unless you enroll your book in Kindle Select and make it unavailable to other packagers and distributors. I advise you not to enroll in the Kindle Select Program, but feel free to ignore me. With the non-USA sites, how much money you get on a sale is difficult to predict exactly because the sale is made in a foreign currency, and a currency exchange has to be made before you can get paid.

There is a "but" to the seventy percent split option. The seventy percent split only applies to book sales made through an Amazon site by a customer within one of twenty countries. These countries include almost all of North America and Europe. If, for instance, a customer from Honduras or Antigua bought your book through the Amazon USA site, you'd only get thirty-five percent on that sale. Why? Let's just chalk this up as one more inexplicable Amazon fact.

Other ebook packagers: If you work with a packager other than these two, the royalty splits may be different from the above. Make sure you investigate how you get paid *before* you sign up with that packager.

Royalty Splits: Print books

Kindle Paperback Books: For your print book, there are a number of possible revenue splits. If your $14.99 book is sold through the USA Amazon site, the split is 35/65 and you'll get $5.25 on each book. If your book is sold through a distributor such as Ingram or Baker & Taylor, you'll get $2.25. Kindle will distribute your book to the European Amazon sites if you let it. And why wouldn't you? For books sold in Europe the exchange rate comes up again, and any revenue figure I quote will change with the currency exchange rate. In a nutshell, your cut will be around $5.25, but it could be higher or lower depending upon you know what.

IngramSpark Print Books: This packager distributes print books to stores and libraries. Calculating the revenue split for a sale is almost impossible because of a number of factors. The factors involved are the discount rate and book returns. Bookstores enjoy a 55% discount rate they can choose to use. If the store discounts your book by the full amount, the sale price is now $8.25. After the store and IngramSpark take their cut, your author compensation isn't very big. The bookstores have the right to return the book if it doesn't sell within a specific time period set by the bookstore. These returns affect your compensation. How much you get paid is calculated by taking the number of books sold minus the book returns. This compensation can actually be a negative number which will lower your compensation in future periods.

Royalty splits: audio books

Royalty splits from audio books are a lot trickier than ebook and print book royalties. The reason is that audio books involve a voice actor who has to be paid in addition to the packager and seller percentages.

There are a few ways to make a deal with the voice actor, and that will vary by audio producer.

Here is the way ACX explains its royalty policy: *ACX authors and publishers can earn between 20%-40% of their title royalties through ACX. The royalty rate you earn is determined by the distribution option you select and the method by which the producer is compensated. For non-exclusive distribution, the rights holder earns a 25% royalty and must compensate the Producer upfront. In an exclusive distribution deal, the rights holder earns a 40% royalty, if compensating the producer upfront. If the rights holder and Producer agree to share royalties, each earns a 20% royalty.*

Here is a link to ACX: https://www.acx.com/help/authors/200484540

Keeping track

As a business, you have to track both your expenses and your income. One very good reason for doing this is because the government will insist upon it.

You need the expense and income data to fill out the Schedule C form for your tax return. This is only for the USA. Different countries will have tax regulations just as complicated as the ones we have.

So how to keep track of this information? You can use an old-fashioned ledger and enter each income or expense item with a pen. You can use a spreadsheet instead of the ledger, or you can buy a software program.

There are a number of accounting programs and tablet apps that can be used for this purpose. *Quicken* by Intuit is a popular program and it has several versions. The one for a business is the most expensive. *Quicken* has editions for both PC's and Mac's. Another choice, for Mac only, is *iBank*, which was recently changed to *Banktivity*. I've used this one for a number of years and it fills my needs. My tax accountant has never had a problem with the reports produced by Banktivity.

Whenever you spend money on your book, enter the expenditure into the program. Whenever a packager sends you royalties, enter it. At the end of the tax year, if the income is larger than the expenses, you owe taxes on the difference. If expenses are larger than income, you have a legitimate tax deduction.

Both programs will allow you to print reports on income versus expense. There are also a number of other reports you can print.

My major income categories are royalties (from book sales), lectures (at libraries and schools), class tuition (for my Udemy classes) and web sales (from my Writers & Authors Resource Center web site)

Most of my expenses are categorized as advertising, promotions, websites and services.

Revenue and expense

If you have a single book published, there isn't much of a problem in determining if the book has recovered all its costs and is making a profit. I have more than twenty books now, not counting the ones that are out of print. I track income and expenses separately for each one in addition to tracking my total income and expenses. Why do I do all this tracking? Because I run a business and I want to know the results for each product I offer. Amazon, Coca-Cola, Goodyear and any company you can think of does the same thing. They track expenses and income for every product they sell in order to determine which ones are the best profit-makers. If a product turns out to be a stinker, they stop carrying it. I've retired a book or two because it wasn't selling, and I didn't want to incur expenses trying to pump up the book sales. I prefer to spend the money on a different book.

I use spreadsheets to track income and expenses on each book. Since I'm a Mac guy, I use Numbers as my spreadsheet program and it works similar to the way Excel works. I use a separate spreadsheet page for each book.

Profit and loss

Let's talk about profit and loss and how to figure out how well you're doing with your book sales. Profit is a simple calculation based on your revenue minus your expenses.

Let's use an example. Suppose you attend a book fair to sell some of your print books. At the end of the day, you sold nine books for $20 each. Your revenue comes to $180. You bought the books from the packager for $45 meaning your net revenue is $135 for the day. Not a bad day's work. But does your book show a profit yet? What about the incurred costs of producing the book? Let's say the cover and a professional editor cost $750, so your book won't show a profit until your net revenue equals or exceeds $750. The equation to calculate this is: net revenue - expenses = profit. If these print books are your only sales so far, the equation is $135 - $750 = -$615. In other words, your profitability is negative. But hey, you recovered a chunk of your expenses. That's how the book selling game goes. You recover your expenses incrementally.

Once your net revenue reaches $750, any additional sales will represent a profit over your embedded book costs. But wait, you say. What about the marketing costs? Good point. You still have to recover those costs.

I break up my costs into two buckets, as I've pointed out before. My initial objective is to recover the costs of getting the book published. Once that happens, then I start repaying the marketing costs. Most of my books (except the most recent ones) have paid back the embedded costs and now I'm working to get back the marketing costs.

Budgets

Budgets allow you to predict and control your expenses and to manage your business. Your expenses will occur in two areas. One is the costs associated with getting a book published. These include such obvious expenses as a cover artist and an editor. There may be some not-so-obvious charges. These can be fees charged by a packager or for an ISBN.

The second area of expenses is marketing costs. Marketing costs will probably be much higher than the publishing costs. Indeed, some marketing costs can be very large. These include hiring a publicist or initiating a publicity campaign and magazine ads.

The main purpose of establishing budgets is to enable you to manage your publishing and marketing plans by selecting options that will fit into the budgets you established. Without a budget and plans, you run the danger of encountering exploding costs, and these can grow almost exponentially.

Authors who are self-publishing a book for the first time often consider publishing and marketing as separate processes or projects. In their view, first you publish the book, and then you start the marketing. This is an erroneous concept. Publishing and marketing are two aspects of a single project and they have to be considered as an entity. The reality is that marketing has to start long before the book is published.

One of the themes behind my *How to Self-publish and Market a Book* is to integrate the publishing and marketing process into a unified project broken up into time frames to spread the workload over six months.

Publishing expense estimates:

If you have already published a book, some of these items will be familiar to you. Keep in mind, these are estimates. If you can do the work yourself, the book design and formatting charges will disappear.

Mandatory Charges:
- Ebook cover: $50+
- Paperback cover: $150+
- Editing: $350 to over $1,000 depending on a range of factors

Possible Charges:

- Packager setup fees: $25-$100
- Distribution fees: $25-$75
- Book design: $50+
- Formatting: $50+
- ISBN: $0 to $125
- Packager conversion services: $150+

Publishing budget notes:

Ebook cover: front cover only.

Print book cover: front, back and spine.

Editing: cost varies with length and your writing skill.

Packager fees: Associated with uploading files. Some packagers will charge a fee, most don't.

Book design: Hiring someone to lay out the interior of the book.

Formatting: Hiring someone to format the book to meet the submission guidelines.

ISBN: The cost of buying an ISBN if the packager doesn't give you one free.

Distribution fees: associated with getting books distributed by Ingram and Baker & Taylor.

Marketing expense estimates:

These costs are all optional in that you don't have to spend money on marketing. The *quid pro quo* here is this: If you don't spend money on marketing, you won't have to worry about reporting royalties to the IRS. You won't have any royalties to report. The sequence of events is this: market first, collect royalties later.

Build your marketing plan based on what you can afford, then select the appropriate tasks.

- Website development: $200 + unless you can do it yourself, then $0.
- Website hosting and URL: $50 per year.
- Website security: $100/year (if you start your own web site, consider this cost to be mandatory)
- Book review services: $25 to $100 each
- Blog tour: $200-$1,000+ depending upon the company used and the length of the tour
- Trailers (similar to movie trailers): $50 to several hundred dollars depending upon length and quality unless you can do it yourself, then $0)

- Print book giveaways: $25-$100
- Social media ads: $25-$100 depending upon the site and the length of the ad.
- Publicist: $4,000 +

Marketing budget notes:

Trailer: a short video about the book.

Website server: a place on the internet where your website/blog lives. An annual fee.

Domain name: the URL used as the internet address for your website/blog. An annual fee.

Blog tours: an organized tour of a number of blog sites.

Taxes

Taxes and breathing
Taxes have similarities to the air we breathe in that both are everywhere. Also, if you don't breathe the air or don't pay your taxes, bad things happen to you.

Schedule C
Royalties from the sale of your book are taxable. They and the expenses incurred during the course of business are reported on Schedule C: Profit or Loss from Business. This form is for use in the United States. If you live in a different country, you'll have to do some research to find the proper form. You can file Schedule C without doing anything special or unique and without even mentioning your company name.

Hobby or business?
If the tax authorities consider your business to be a hobby, it will limit the expenses you can deduct. To remedy this possibility, you can apply for a separate tax ID number for your company.

Why bother with this tax ID nonsense? Having a tax ID and a company name grants you some legitimacy with the Internal Revenue Service. A tax ID along with a company name will help convince them that you're a serious writer/author and that you are indeed a legitimate business.

After you send in the SS-4 form, eventually you'll get a response with your unique tax ID number. It looks different from your Social Security number, which is also a tax ID number.

Selling print books
One of the functions of a publisher (or a packager if you're self-published) is to collect financial data about your book sales. They'll distribute your royalties, usually once a month. They will also file tax forms listing your royalties and taxes paid, if any.

However, a different situation arises when you have a print book and you sell copies of it at a book fair or a lecture or a library reading. Almost every state has a sales tax, so how do you collect these sales taxes? The answer is: Maybe you don't!

In order to sell a print copy of your book, you had to order the copy from your publisher or packager. If you ordered the books from Kindle, they charged you sales tax on your order. In this case you don't have to charge sales tax when you resell the book. If you ordered print books from a different packager, check on whether or not you were charged sales tax. If you weren't, then you will be responsible for collecting the tax when you resell the book. Tax laws vary greatly by state. Check with your state tax authority to learn about the relevant regulations.

If you reside in a country with a VAT, you'll have to do a bit of research to figure out how to comply with the VAT regulations.

Breaking even

Overview

A break even analysis is a vital tool that allows you to understand the risks involved in funding a project or a marketing campaign. Marketing campaigns can be used to achieve two important goals. One is extending your name recognition. The second is to increase sales. Trailers can be used for the first goal. A trailer may not sell many books, but it can make readers acquainted with you as the author and with your book, and that is a good thing. Initiating a marketing campaign frequently involves money. These expenditures should be viewed as an investment and as such should be expected to bring in a return on the investment. That's fancy business talk meaning you should get your invested money back and then some.

Break even templates

Before spending the upfront money for the marketing campaign, you can run a break even analysis to see if you have a snowball's chance of recovering your investment. There is an easy way to do this using spreadsheet templates. The templates are already configured and all you have to do is plug in the numbers.

The new version of Numbers spreadsheet program (for Mac computers) comes with a break even template. MS Excel also has a similar pre-built spreadsheet. Here is a link to a site where you download an Excel template: http://office.microsoft.com/en-us/templates/break-even-analysis-tc001017515.asp

Example

As an example, let's say you come across this attractive marketing site. Here's the deal. For an upfront price of $150, the site will advertise your book for two weeks, but the book price must be reduced to half-price or less. To simplify the example, we'll restrict sales to your D2D packager with its seventy percent royalty. Your book normally sells for $3.99 and you want to see break even points for prices of $1.99 (50% discount) and $1.49 (63% discount).

The Numbers spreadsheet has an item called Variable Cost per Unit that has to be factored in. This is frequently called Cost of Sales. In the case of your book, this is the amount of the sale D2D collects from each book sale. With the $1.99 price option, the cost of sales is $.60 per book and for the $1.49 price option, it's $.45.

If you run the analysis, it shows that with the $1.99 price option and a fixed cost of $150 (the cost of the marketing campaign) you have to sell 108 copies of the book to break even. Every book sale over 108 will produce a profit for you on this ad campaign. For instance, if you sell 160 copies your revenue will be $318 with a cost of $246 netting a profit of $72. This spreadsheet analysis is pasted below. You can see the components and the graph showing costs and sales. The numbers in the yellow section are the variables you have to enter for your study.

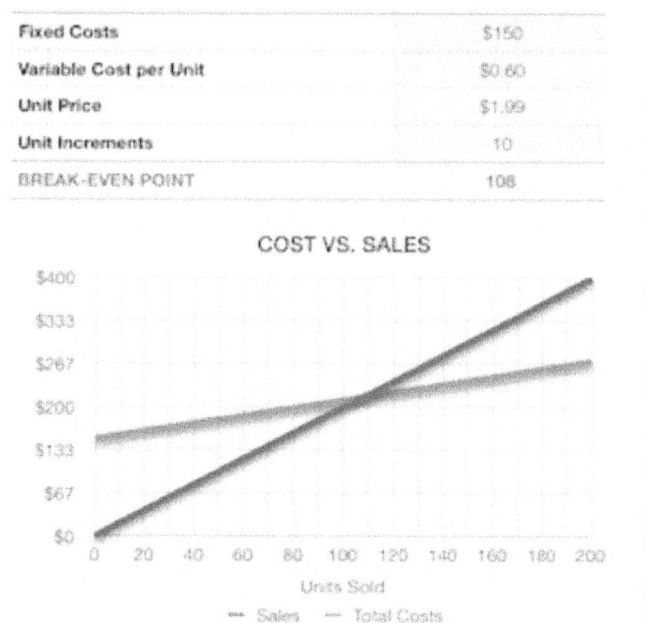

Analysis

The beauty of a spreadsheet like this is that it is simple to run another analysis for the $1.49 option. Adjusting the data for the new study yields these results. You have to sell 144 books to recover the $150 upfront charge. If you manage to sell 200 copies, the results are: $298 in book sales, $240 in costs, leaving a profit of $58.

After you run the break even analyses, you're left to answer this question: Can I sell 108 (or 144) copies of my book? Much of the answer depends on the site that provides the marketing campaign. If it has enough clout to reach a large number of potential book buyers — in your genre — then the answer is: yes, you can reach the break even point and beyond. On the other hand, if the site is obscure with no real clout — or promotes to the general population — then the answer is: no, you'll probably lose your shirt on this deal.

Implications

This type of analysis has implications. In many cases, the company running the promotion is making big bucks while you are struggling to break even. In the example above, you are paying the promotion site $150 to send out emails to its client list and to put your book prominently on its website. Still, this can be a good way to get your book into the hands of many readers who otherwise would have never heard of you or your book.

This example demonstrates that like almost everything in marketing, it is fraught with financial peril.

Be cautious. Be very cautious!

Start a publishing company?

What?
If you plan to self-publish more than one or two books, maybe it's time to upgrade that book selling company to a publishing company. Upgrading won't change anything about the book selling operations, but having a publishing company will increase your presence in the publishing world.

Pros and cons
There are a number of pros and cons involved in establishing your own publishing company.

Pros
- Lessens the self-publishing stigma (slightly).
- Allows you to work with publishing organizations that won't deal with authors (especially self-publishing authors).
- Allows you to brag that you now have a publisher for your books.
- Your company can be registered through Bowker to establish legitimacy.

Cons
- Costs money.
- Doesn't necessarily increase book sales and revenue.

Pros
Lessens the self-publishing stigma (slightly): Let's face it: there is still a stigma attached to self-publishing. You'll frequently hear snide comments that the author wasn't good enough to get a publisher to buy his book and that's why the book is self-published. Much of the bad reputation self-publishing has developed comes from the fact that self-publishing has become too easy. People who have no writing skills write and publish the first draft of a book with hand-drawn covers.

Starting your own imprint will impress other self-publishing authors and will identify you as one who is willing to take risks. The other authors will immediately want to know if the company is open for submissions. This issue is really of minor consequence.

Allows you to work with publishing organizations that won't deal with authors (especially self-publishing authors):
This one is much more important than the previous one. Part of this issue is an off-shoot of the self-publishing stigma, but it is also an integral part of the publishing business. Some organizations simply won't deal with authors but will work with publishing companies. There are many, many more authors than publishers, and working only with the publishers cuts down on the number of entities that have to be dealt with. And many authors are prima donnas who expect special treatment. Publishers, on the other hand, are businesses that presumably won't carry on the way authors do. One such organization is the Independent Book Publishers Association (IBPA).

Allows you to brag that you now have a publisher for your books: This is not an inconsequential issue. At public appearances, people will ask if you are self-published. Rattling off the name of the publisher who puts out your books impresses many people. Having a publisher also makes your books more interesting since everyone has bought a self-published book that turned out to be a stinker. Since you have a publisher, that implies to many people that the book went through a vetting process and can't be as bad as that stinker.

Your company can be registered through Bowker to establish legitimacy: Bowker (the ISBN company) maintains a registry of publishers. If you start your own publishing company, you can file a form on the Bowker website and get registered.

Cons

Costs money: You really didn't expect an opportunity like this to be free, did you? The Bowker registration will cost money. A new domain name for your publishing company website will result in an annual fee. You'll also need new business cards.

Doesn't necessarily increase book sales and revenue: Just because you have a publishing company doesn't mean people will rush out to buy your books. As with self-publishing, no one knows about your books or your company until you tell them. You still have to do all the marketing and self-promotion.

Book publisher associations

As a publisher, you can join various associations and organizations that authors can't join. These groups have contacts within the publishing industry that can help you spread the word about your books. For instance, they have lists of thousands of book stores and more lists identifying libraries all over the country. You would have a great deal of trouble and a lot of hard work to identify even a fraction of these book stores and libraries on your own.

There are a number of publishers associations such as Independent Book Publishers Association (IBPA), the Association of American Publishers (AAP), the Association of Publishers for Special Sales (APSS). There are other associations organized around a small geographical location, such as a state. A search engine will give you a lengthy list of these organizations.

As with everything else in life (and especially publishing and book marketing), dig into the details before committing money to join up. Some associations are worth the money while some will look dubious and offer little value for the money.

Resources

Links

IRS forms: http://www.irs.gov/Forms-&-Pubs

Advantages & Disadvantages of sole proprietorship: http://www.nytimes.com/allbusiness/AB4113314_primary.html

Advantages and Disadvantages of Limited Liability Companies: http://www.rocketlawyer.com/article/why-start-an-llc-limited-liability-company-advantages-and-disadvantages.rl

SBA business planning tool: sba.gov/business-plan

Independent Book Publishers Association (IBPA): https://www.ibpa-online.org

Find better software: https://www.capterra.com

Books

The Ultimate Startup Book, Kevin Duncan, et al. John Murray Press

Book Marketing Fundamentals, Hank Quense. Strange Worlds Publishing

How to Write a Business Plan, Alex Genadinik. Semantic Valley LLC

Business Basics For Authors, Hank Quense. Strange Worlds Publishing

Publishing

Table of Contents
Publishing overview   90
Traditional publishing.   95
Self-publishing action plan.   98
 Step 1 Editing.   104
 Step 2: Covers.   106
 Step 3:Formatting.   108
 Step 4: Book description.   111
 Step 5: Packager accounts.   114
 Step 6: Book blurb.   118
 Step 7: Description.   122
 Step 8: Keywords.   124
 Step 9: Categories.   126
 Step 10: Price.   129

Publishing overview

Manuscript status

Is your manuscript finished? If it's a first draft, it most definitely is not finished. In this case, your manuscript is filled with typos, misspellings and outright mistakes. Ernest Hemingway, who won a Pulitzer Prize, once said, "The first draft of anything is a piece of s—t." My first drafts qualify for this statement, and so do yours. No one sees my stuff until at least the third draft and sometimes not until the fourth or fifth draft.

The objective of self-publishing is to surround your manuscript with a quality book package. Creating a quality book package for a first draft is a waste of time because the content is junk.

So how many drafts will it take to finish the manuscript? It's 'done' when you feel you can't improve it any more. If you don't find any mistakes or typos and you don't get an urge to rewrite a paragraph or a scene, it's as good as you can make it. However, just because you don't see any mistakes does not mean beta readers and a professional editor won't find problems.

For some writers, letting go is a traumatic event; they want to continue to revise and revise still more. To these writers, the book never seems 'done.' When writers continue to revise a book, they'll reach a point where their efforts are detrimental to the work: they are actually dis-improving the book.

Eventually, the writer has to take a leap of faith and decide the book is 'done.' Then it's time to move on.

Time frames

The recommended time frame for a publishing and marketing project is six months. If this is your first self-publishing project, you may think the interval is absurd. However, to produce a quality book package with quality content takes time. It also involves other people, and their time has to be factored into the interval. Professionals such as cover artists and editors have other clients, not just you. To get your project worked on you may have to wait in queue until the other clients are taken care of. This delay has to be included in the project interval.

Lack of commonality

A further complication for new authors is this: planning and writing the book does nothing to prepare the author for the publishing and marketing parts of the project. Planning, writing, publishing and marketing involve four completely different skill sets and the only commonality is that all four phases involve the same book.

What type of book

One of the early decisions a self-publishing author has to make concerns what type of book will be published. Ebook? Print book? Both?

Ebook formats: Ebooks come in different flavors to satisfy different e-reader devices. The primary ones today are described below.

PDF format: This file type has been around for a long time. It stands for Portable Document Format and is used to read documents on a computer monitor. Tablets and phones can now view this format file type. PDF produces a file that is almost identical to the original file that created it. The advantage of the PDF file (over a Word file, for instance) is the PDF file can't be changed while a word processor file can be altered. Modern software does allow the PDF file to be marked up (with corrections or annotations), but the original text can't be changed.

EPub format: This is the world-wide standard for ebooks. Formatting a document to be published in this format can be an exasperating experience because of the stringent standards that have been developed. Most word processors assume whatever you type into the computer will be printed, hence their default settings support printing the document. Many of these default settings violate Epub3 standards, hence the need to spend time on formatting the ebook manuscript. More on this issue later on.

Other formats: There are other ebook formats, such as HTML to mention one; however, most self-publishing authors will rarely, if ever, need to use them.

Print book formats: Print books come in paperback and hardcover styles. The latter are more expensive to produce and hence will demand a higher price. Print books also come in a variety of sizes that you'll have to specify in order to have your cover match the book size. My novels all are 5.5 inches by 8.5 inches. Other possible sizes are: 6x9 and 8.5x11. There are dozens of sizes available in both US and metric measurements.

Audiobooks: Once your ebook or print book is completed, you have the option of having an audiobook edition created. This will involve hiring a voice artist to read and record the text.

Comparison list

As you might expect, there are a number of advantages and disadvantages in publishing one or the other type of book or both types. For that reason I compiled this comparison list. It shows the pros and cons for print books and ebooks. I'm sure there are many more bullet items that can be added under each header, but these are the major ones to my way of thinking.

Ebooks: Plus
- Less expensive covers
- Faster publication cycle
- Instant global distribution
- Instant download and availability
- No book production costs
- Author gets higher percentage of sales revenue (on a lower book price)

Ebooks: Negative
- Many readers don't like ebooks and prefer to read a print book
- Some ebook seller sites are reader-hostile in that they are difficult to navigate
- Difficult to sell at book fairs and other personal appearances
- Book prices will generally be much lower than print book prices resulting in lower revenue per sale

Print: Plus
- Can be given as gifts to family and friends
- Can be sold at book fairs, etc.
- Bookstore sales possible
- Library sales possible

Print: Negative
- More expensive cover

- Slower distribution
- Distribution may be restricted geographically
- More expensive production costs
- Distributor sales suck up almost all the revenue leaving little for the author
- Bookstore returns can be a problem

As you can see from the list, ebooks and print books do have significant differences.

Useful links

Check these links for more information on publishing options

https://www.tckpublishing.com/complete-guide-to-publishing-services-for-writers/

https://blog.reedsy.com/scams-and-publishing-companies-to-avoid/

Publishing options

Today, an author has a number of options on how the book gets published. A brief description of each is listed here.

Major publishing houses: This option is the dream of almost all authors in the beginning. Many of these require an agent to submit. While desirable, this option can take years to publish the book if successful.

Independent publishing houses: There are many of these publishers and they are generally easier to link up with. Most of them don't require an agent and they are much faster to publish than the big guys.

Hybrid publishers: These are relatively new. While they have some legitimate features such as editing services and cover production, other services are similar to vanity presses in that the author pays the publisher to publish the book.

Vanity publishers: These publishers will accept your book without question provided you can afford to pay their fees. The fees are enormous. Think thousands of dollars. The publisher will also attempt to convince you to enroll in quite expensive marketing programs.

Self-publishing: This option is increasingly popular with authors. With this option, the author has to do all the work a publisher would do.

Be warned: Writing a book does nothing to prepare you for the tasks associated with self-publishing. It is arduous and expensive. Still, thousands of authors do it, so why can't you?

Traditional publishing

The traditional publishing process consists of researching agents and publishers, scouring their submission guidelines, developing submission packages, submitting them and waiting. And waiting. And waiting.

Submission package
Every agent and publisher will have submission guidelines on their website and each one will list different requirements.

Find those guidelines and follow them exactly.

All of them will require a query cover letter and a synopsis. They may also require an author bio and a chapter or two from the book.

Query cover letter
The query letter is an important part of the submission package to both an agent and a publisher. However, each submission package will have different requirements for the letter.

Here is a link to help you fashion an effective letter: https://aalitagents.org/

Synopsis
The synopsis is one of the most difficult things to write. Think about it: you wrote a book, perhaps 80,000 words, and now you have to re-write it using only a few pages.

Here are links to help you write one:

Fiction:
https://www.janefriedman.com/how-to-write-a-novel-synopsis/

Non-fiction: https://www.tckpublishing.com/nonfiction-book-synopsis/

A final word of advice about a synopsis. Many authors use the synopsis to market the book. This is a mistake! Every synopsis ever written is boring to read. A synopsis has its uses but marketing isn't one of them. More on this topic later on.

Agents

Agents are a necessary route to some of the biggest publishers. There are many, many agents in the world, but most of them limit their activity to specific genres. Use the links below to find agents who deal with your type of book. Add more notes as required. Be sure to follow the agent's submission guidelines exactly.

There are entire books written about how to write query letters and book proposals. Go to Amazon and search for 'query letters' to see what I'm talking about. Here is a link to an informative article on these matters. https://www.janefriedman.com/query-letters-nonfiction-memoir/

Agent links
https://www.pw.org/literary_agents

https://aalitagents.org

Agent queries

Keep track of your agent queries in your notebook using a format such as this one:

Agent name:
Email:
Query date:
Response:

Agent name:
Email:
Query date
Response:

Publishers

Some major publishers and most independent publishers do not require an agent in order to submit a book or a book proposal. There are a large number of publishers you can contact.

Here are links to a list of publishers.

https://www.tckpublishing.com/list-of-book-publishers/

https://www.publishersglobal.com/directory/united-states/publishers-in-united-states

Many publishers specialize in that they only publish certain types of books. Be sure your queries take this into account. Be sure to follow the publisher's submission guidelines exactly.

Keep track of your publisher queries in your notebook using a format such as this one:

Publisher's name:
Email:
Query date:
Response:

Publisher's name:
Email:
Query date:
Response:

You probably won't need the snail mail address for the agents and publishers since manuscripts and queries are sent via email these days.

Self-publishing action plan

Self-publishing tidbits

Before we get into the action plan, there are a few topics to discuss and understand.

Common self-publishing misconceptions

Self-publishing a book for the first time can be a daunting project because it presents two problems to the new author. The first is that writing a book doesn't prepare you for the publishing work which requires a skill set that is quite different from writing the book. The second problem is research. The internet is filled with inaccurate information and in some cases, erroneous information. Encouragement to publish your book The Lazy Way is an example of this erroneous information.

So what is The Lazy Way?

On Monday, you finish the manuscript (an early unedited draft).

On Tuesday, you hand draw a cover.

On Wednesday, you upload the stuff to Kindle.

On Thursday, you celebrate because you are a 'published' author.

Here is an example of The Lazy Way and what you may find on the web. I once read a post from a writer who put up a message like this on LinkedIn: "I finished writing my manuscript. Now what do I do?" Someone answered with, "Upload it to Kindle. It's easy." This is the worst possible advice you could possibly get. It recommended that the writer publish the book The Lazy Way.

I'll make three comments about advice like this. If this manuscript was uploaded to Kindle, no one would buy it or read it because it's a piece of garbage. Books published this way are the reason self-publishing has a bad reputation. People who make recommendations like this have no concept of what self-publishing means.

What self-publishing means is the self-publishing author must do all the work a publishing house would do if the author had sold his manuscript to it.

This is self-publishing the professional way. In short, that means getting a unique cover, having the manuscript professionally edited and formatting the ebook.

This last task confuses many inexperienced self-publishing authors. What they see on their computer screen is suitable for a print edition of a book but requires a number of changes before it can become a correctly formatted ebook.

Here is a few of these formatting changes:
- No page numbers
- No page breaks
- No paragraph indenting using the tab key or the space bar
- No centering using the space bar or the tab key.

With ebooks, the indenting must use the indent command, not the space bar or the tab key, and centering must be done with the alignment command.

Another issue has to do with marketing. Understanding who the book's customers are isn't as straightforward as one may think. For instance, if you authored a children's picture book, you may think the customers are the kids. But kids don't have money or credit cards. Kids don't browse in bookstores and on the web. So, the customers for a picture book are the kid's parents, grandparents and other family members. When it comes to book marketing, your marketing plan has to start with a strategic plan. Identifying the customers is just one aspect in that plan.

Finally, aspiring self-publishing authors will soon run into scammers who "offer" service packages to help the author format the book, publish the book, market the book, etc. The simple fact is that the scammers swarm all over the web looking for new authors who are struggling to understand how to publish and market their book. Fending them off is a constant concern.

Although the issues mentioned do exist, thousands of other self-publishing authors have successfully published their book and so can you. It helps enormously, however, to be aware of these issues as you start your self-publishing journey.

Print on demand (POD)

Print on Demand, or POD as it is usually called, is a process that is used to fulfill print book orders. It is used extensively by the indie press houses and all the packagers you'll come across.

The way the traditional publishers operate is that they print thousands of books at one time and ship them to warehouses in advance of the book's release date. From there, the books are distributed to bookstores. This is an expensive way to do business and it only fits the business model of the big boys. The small publishers and packagers need a different business model and POD suits their needs perfectly.

In effect, what POD means is that copies of your print book don't physically exist until someone places an order for a copy. There are no shelves filled with your books waiting for someone to buy one. Once an order is received, the cover and manuscript files are printed, packaged and sent to the customer.

With modern computer-controlled printing machines, the POD book can be printed almost instantly. Most orders can be fulfilled within a day or two.

Pre-orders

Just because you uploaded the book to the packagers doesn't mean the book is available. If you set the publication for sometime in the future, the ebook will fall into a pre-order status. D2D and Kindle allow and encourage pre-orders.

There are a number of benefits to establishing a pre-order. For instance, you can advertise the book. You can update the Amazon Central listing. You can list it on Goodreads and other book sites. You can request reviews; however, the reviews can't be posted while the book is in pre-order. Only after the book becomes available will reviews be allowed.

If a reader purchases your pre-order, the book will be delivered on the release date.

One marketing tactic you can use to promote pre-orders is to show a reduced price that will be valid until the release date, at which time you raise the price. For instance, if the full price will be $2.99, you can show a pre-order price for $1.99.

Pre-orders only apply to ebooks, not to print books.

Publishing budget

Your publishing budget has two mandatory items and a number of other items that may or may not require funding. The two mandatory items are a book cover and professional editing.

Book covers are important because in many cases the first contact a buyer has with your book is seeing the cover on some website like Amazon, and then it most likely will be a small icon.

A dull cover will not grab that buyer's attention. A unique cover is likely to get the buyer to look more closely at your book.

Editing will be the largest expense in the publishing project.

Other expenses such as formatting and book design may not occur if you have the technical expertise to do it yourself or have a software program to help out.

An ISBN may be required. If so, it can cost a chunk of money in the United States. ISBN stands for International Standard Book Number. Oftentimes, however, it is possible to get a free ISBN.

Here is a list of budget estimates for the publishing end of your project. Note the emphasis on the word estimates.

Mandatory charges:
- Ebook cover: $50+
- Print cover: $150+
- Editing: $350 to over $1,000 depending on a range of factors

Possible charges:
- Distribution fees: $25-$75
- Book design: $50+
- Formatting: $50+
- ISBN: $0 to $125

If you plan on publishing an ebook and a print book, the covers will cost less than the sum of the two covers shown above. This is because the ebook cover is also the front of the print book cover.

If you plan an ebook and a print book, you'll need two ISBNs. You'll need additional ISBNs for hardcover and audiobook editions.

Publishing task list

Self-publishing a book is a complex project with a number of tasks that must be worked on. I use a spreadsheet to help me manage and track my progress on the project. It can also be used to track my costs. The graphic shows the spreadsheet layout.

Publishing Task List			
Task	Status	Funding required?	Cost
INTIAL TASKS			
Manuscript Status	0%	no	
Beta Readers	0%	no	
Publishing budget	0%	no	
PROFESSIONAL HELP			
Cover artist	0%	yes	$0
Professional Editor	0%	yes	$0

You can create your own version using the list of topics below.

INITAL TASKS
Manuscript Status
Beta Readers
Publishing budget

PROFESSIONAL HELP
Cover artist
Professional Editor
Other help

BOOK DESCRIPTION
Keywords
Book Blurb
Book Description
Price

GETTING READY
Packagers
Manuscript preparation
Getting an ISBN

PRE-LAUNCH ACTIVITIES
Establish launch date
Upload the files
Pre-order
Total Costs

Step 1: Editing

Professional editing

Getting a professional editor to work on your book is not an option; it is a mandatory requirement! An editor provides another pair of eyes to read and polish your manuscript.

You may think your manuscript is perfect, but it isn't. It doesn't matter how many times you went through it to dig out typos and to polish sentences, it still needs an editor.

Four types of editors

Developmental editors help with story line, character development and plot. These are the most expensive types of editors. If you use this type, it should have been done long before you started the publishing process because you will have a lot of revisions to take care of. If you use a developmental editor, you can skip the beta reader task, but you still need a second editor to correct the typos and clumsy sentence structure. Many of these issues came about when you revised the book from a developmental editor's suggestions or from beta reader changes.

Line editors provide comprehensive help and will look at plot, sentence structure, dialogue, word usage, and multiple other issues. Beta readers will do some of these functions, and if you have a competent team of them you most likely won't need this type of editor.

Copy editors will find a lot of mistakes you missed. These include typos, incorrect usage ('too' instead of 'to' or 'two'). A good editor will also find clumsy sentence structure, repeated words and other mistakes.

Proof readers are similar to copy editors. They will find typos, grammar errors and check for complete sentences and the occasional wrong word usage, but they don't look at your clumsy sentences or bad dialogue.

Editing

At an absolute minimum your book will require copy editing. If your errors are not rooted out, the reader will think she bought a book written by an amateur. If you want to produce quality content, it has to be professionally edited. Always remember, your name will be on the title page and the cover, so you want the book to be as perfect as possible.

More on editing

Editing will be the most expensive cost in your publishing process. Make sure you account for this in your budget.

You should get the editing underway as early as possible because it will take time for the editor to do her job, especially if she has other projects in front of yours.

The usual result of an editor's work is you get a marked-up manuscript filled with highlighted typos and suggested edits.

You can ease the revision process by asking the editor to return each chapter as it is finished. This will spread out the revision process.

One final word about editors: It's your book and you don't have to accept everything the editor says.

Step 2: Covers

Covers in general

A unique book cover is an important element in getting your book noticed. Studies have shown that many readers are initially attracted to a book by the cover. Consequently, a shoddy cover won't attract potential readers. Look at a book page on Amazon. The first thing you'll see is the cover image. This image can go a long way towards attracting a buyer's attention.

My advice is to hire a competent cover artist to create a cover for your book. If you already know such an artist, great. In this case, you may be able to get a cover at an attractive price. If you don't know such an artist or if you can't afford a hefty expense, the question comes down to this: How do you find someone who can produce the cover for your book? The usual way to find such an artist is to use the internet.

A web search can produce a slew of names for artists willing to work on your book. I don't recommend contacting any of these names right away. Why? There is a possibility that some of the names aren't legitimate artists but are rather scammers hoping to get contacted to make some money. Other names will be mediocre artists who will oversell their ability. Instead, do a web search on the artist's name to see if there any red flags associated with the name.

You can also ask your social media contacts for names of cover artists they've used in the past.

Pre-made covers

In your web searches, you'll find the names of artists who have produced a number of pre-made ebook covers you can buy at an inexpensive price. Once you pay for it, the artist will add your title and name to the cover and send it to you. While this may sound like an ideal solution, it comes with a few drawbacks. First, the covers are generic and won't match your story very well. Second, a generic cover may tell the potential buyer the content will also be generic. Third, the artist retains the copyright to the cover blank and can sell it again to another author. So there is a strong possibility you will see 'your' cover on someone else's book.

Print covers

Print covers are more complicated than ebook covers. With ebooks, you only need a graphic for the front cover. Print book covers, on the other hand, have three parts: the front cover (same as the ebook cover), a back cover and a spine between the two. In addition, print books come in a number of sizes, and the size must be determined before you can get a cover.

Print cover spines

The spine is the tricky part. The width of the spine has to be calculated, and that width depends upon how many pages are in the book and the thickness of the paper used. Packagers have a standard page thickness which will be shown somewhere on their website, and you can use that number to calculate the spine thickness by using a spine calculator. One such calculator can be found at: https://www.bookmobile.com/book-spine-width-calculator/. Book packagers like Kindle and IngramSpark have a calculator that allows you to come up with the correct figure. Once you get the thickness number, save it because your cover artist needs it to produce the cover.

The final print cover will be in pdf format and will be ready to upload to your packager, who will merge it with your text file. It looks a bit weird when you see one for the first time. On the left side of the file is the back cover. In the middle is the spine, and the front cover is on the right side of the graphic. On the back cover, notice the unused space at the lower right corner next to the spine. This is where the bar code and the ISBN go. The packager will add this when the book is printed.

Print book size

Book size is a matter of preference and there are a lot of sizes to choose from. You'll have to select a book size before the print book cover can be completed.

Step 3: Formatting

If you plan to publish both an ebook and a print book, you'll have to format two different versions of your manuscript, and the versions will be quite different.

If you format a file for a print book and then upload it to an ebook packager, you will end up with an ebook that is mostly unreadable. In the case of the Draft2Digital packager, your file will be instantly rejected because of incorrect formatting. Similarly, a file formatted for an ebook and sent to a print packager will result in a mess.

Print book formatting

Formatting the print book is straightforward. Make sure you use a copy of the master manuscript for this task, not the master itself.

Your word processor assumes whatever you wrote will be printed so the program's default settings support a print edition. What you see on the computer screen is pretty much what the print book will look like.

The biggest chore right now is to ensure the manuscript is uniform. Review it and correct any inconsistencies. With that done, you're ready to move on to the print book layout task.

Before you format the copy make any appropriate size changes necessary. (See Step 4)

Ebook formatting

This task is radically different from the print book formatting. Much of the work here comes about because your word processor is set up for document printing. Many of those pesky defaults are not acceptable for ebooks, which have to be formatted in accordance with the Epub3 Standard.

To begin the formatting, eliminate the headers and footers. This will, of course, eliminate your page numbers. One aspect of ebooks is that page numbers become irrelevant because e-readers can adjust the type of font and the size of the font. This ability to change fonts makes page numbers extraneous. Any page numbers you see in an ebook reader were added by that ebook reader software.

Next, eliminate all page breaks and replace them with three blank lines. Ebooks can't have page breaks, so if your master manuscript had a page break after the end of each chapter, the page break has to be replaced. If you don't remove the page breaks, they will be eliminated by the packager's software, and that can lead to unpredictable results.

That takes care of the easy part.

Epub3 requirements

The Epub3 Standard has stringent requirements, and ebook packagers demand adherence to the standard.

The ebook formatting process can be a complicated and frustrating chore. Fortunately, there is an excellent book on how to format an ebook in accordance with the Epub3 Standard. It's called the *Smashwords Style Guide* and its author is Mark Coker, the Smashwords founder and president. It's free and you can download a copy here: https://www.smashwords.com/books/view/52

Ebook table of contents

Still another task with ebooks involves the Table of Contents. It has to be hyperlinked to the appropriate places in the manuscript. (Did I mention before that the Epub3 Standard was written for the readers, not the authors?) What this means is that if a reader clicks or touches Chapter 3 in the Table of Contents, the reader will instantly jump to the start of Chapter 3.

In brief, the way you establish these hyperlink jumps is to go through the manuscript and bookmark each chapter heading. Back in the Table of Contents, you then establish a hyperlink from the chapter listing to the associated bookmark. The Smashwords Style Guide has much more detail on this topic.

Your packager *may* hyperlink the Table of Contents, but there is no guarantee the packager will do it correctly. I prefer to do it myself and test each link to ensure it works properly.

Embedded links

With an ebook, you can embed a link into the text like this: my website. When a reader clicks or touches the link, she will go to the website behind the link. This scheme doesn't work with print books. Here you have to display the link like this: my website can be found at https://writersarc.com

In this case, the reader will have to type the link into a browser search box or address bar.

Other help

If you have trouble formatting an ebook or designing the interior, you may need to hire additional help. You may need this help if you simply don't have the time to spend on these chores.

Once again this is where your Goodreads and LinkedIn contacts can come in handy. Ask for names and emails of experienced people in these fields. Be sure to ask for references to avoid getting scammed.

Smashwords has a list of authors who may be willing to do the formatting and design work for a fee. These authors do not work for Smashwords, they simply know how to do this stuff. You can find this list at: https://www.smashwords.com/list

Step 4: Book design

Book design refers to the layout of the interior of the book. Print books and ebooks will have different layouts.

Most of this section deals with print books.

Print book size

With print books, your big decision is to decide on the size of your published book. If you go to a library or bookstore and look around, you'll see that books come in a variety of sizes. Your book packager will allow you to select the book size from more than a dozen different sizes. My paperback novels are 5.5 inches by 8.5 inches. Why? No special reason. It seemed like a good size when I published my first book and subsequent books are the same size so they match on a bookshelf.

Once you decide on a size, you need to change the print master file pages to that size and establish margins on the top, bottom and both sides.

With the size issue out of the way, you can now deal with margins. The left side (inside) margin will have to be different from the right side margin because of the spine and cover. For instance, if your book has between 151 and 400 pages, the left (inside) margin has to be .375 inches while the right (outside) margin must be at least .25 inches but can be greater. The margins can be set on the word processor page used to establish the page size.

Once you've changed the book size, you'll notice the book has changed significantly. Not the least of the changes is the number of pages has increased, possibly appreciably. Make a note of the page count. You'll need this number to calculate the spine width.

The size change can have an impact on the book layout. For instance, if you started each chapter on a new page, you may find there is now a blank page or two in the book, and you'll have to make adjustments to remove them.

Warning: changing the size of the print book will affect the formatting of the book. Make sure you take this into account and update the formatting.

The size change may cause any graphics to move to different locations. Spend time reviewing the manuscript to make any necessary adjustments.

Kindle has a help page on cover design with information on spine calculations. You can find it at: https://kdp.amazon.com/en_US/help/topic/G201857950.

Provide your cover artist with this spine width measurement so he can produce a properly sized cover for your book. Don't do the spine width calculations until you finish the rest of the book design. Your choices can change the number of pages in the print book.

Fonts

One of the basic decisions you'll make is the font that you'll be using. There are many font families to choose from, and which one you use is a personal decision. I generally use Verdana font.

Choosing a font can have economic repercussions for print books. Some fonts need more space than other fonts. The more space a font uses, the more pages a book will have. More pages means higher production costs. In other words, you, the publisher, have to balance the attractiveness of the font with the costs of producing a copy of the book.

In similar fashion, the size of the font used also affects the production costs. Obviously, a twelve point font will require more pages than a ten point font will. If you go for a small font size to lower production costs, you start to affect the readability of the book. Is the type so small that some potential readers won't buy it because they can't read it?

With ebooks, the font family and font size are mostly irrelevant. Once a reader has the ebook on her tablet, she can change the font family and the font size to suit her own tastes.

Line spacing

Line spacing is another parameter that can affect the number of print pages. No matter what spacing you use to write the book, either double-space or one-and-a-half space, change it to single space. This is the accepted standard for print books.

Headers & footers

With headers and footers (for print books, not ebooks), use one or the other. I use only headers. That's where the page number goes and you can put the book's title there if you wish.

Cheat sheets

To ensure the crucially important uniformity of my book design, I write everything down on a sheet of paper, essentially a cheat sheet. This is so I don't inadvertently change stuff in the middle of the book. The cheat sheet has the font family, the size of chapter headings (eighteen point), section size (fourteen point), the size of the text (twelve point), how many spaces between chapters (three lines), the spaces between sections (two spaces) and any other design information.

Step 5: Packagers

In this chapter, I list information on three packagers. There are many more than these three but these are the ones I recommend you use. If you want to use others, read ALL of the fine print before committing your book to that packager.

Kindle

In the publishing world, Kindle is the 800 pound gorilla in the room. Most of your book sales will come from Amazon.

You can create an account using this link: https://kdp.amazon.com/en_US/

With Kindle you can publish your book in both ebook and print editions. Books published using Kindle will show up on Amazon sites worldwide. (Before you ask, when your book shows up on the Amazon site in Japan, it is not translated into Japanese.)

Starting an account is straight forward.

Amazon/Kindle will distribute print books to other sites such as Barnes & Noble. Ebooks however, will only be distributed within the Amazon universe.

Kindle will provide a free ISBN for your print book if you wish. It doesn't use ISBNs for ebooks.

Draft2Digital

This packager merged with Smashwords and distributes ebooks to many sites that Amazon does not. These sites include libraries and many international book distributors. You can find D2D here: https://www.draft2digital.com

Recently, D2D announced it will soon begin distributing print books.

D2D will provide free ISBNs for your books if you wish.

IngramSpark

IngramSpark is a large packager and distributor that deals mainly with bookstores. If you want to have a chance of seeing your self-published print book in bookstores, you'll have to use IngramSpark as a print book packager because bookstores will not deal with Amazon print books for several reasons. A main reason is because Amazon will not allow book returns from the bookstores and that is a deal breaker for them.

If you want to use IngramSpark, you'll have to furnish them with an ISBN for your book. You can find the site here: https://www.ingramspark.com

You can use both IngramSpark and Amazon to distribute print books at the same time and you can use the same ISBN for both packagers.

Be warned, the IngramSpark site is notoriously user-unfriendly.

Getting paid

When the book is sold, you don't get paid immediately. You will eventually, but you'll have to wait a while. Most packagers distribute royalties once a month. Before you can get paid, you'll have to set up channels that allow the packager to disburse the money to you. Some of the options include a PayPal deposit or a direct deposit to a bank account. These last two are known as Electronic Funds Transfer (EFT). Which option your packager wants you to use will be found somewhere on its website along with instructions on how to set it up.

Want a royalty check mailed to your home? Forget about it! That is sooooo 20th Century.

ISBN

ISBNs in the United States can only be bought from Bowker https://www.bowker.com

If you live in Canada, you can get a free ISBN from the government,

A single ISBN costs $125. A block of ten ISBNs consists $295.

Packagers like D2D buy ISBNs in bundles of a thousand, and this reduces the price to around a dollar each. This means if you accept a free ISBN from D2D, the number identifies D2D, not you, as the publisher. The D2D official wording with the ISBN reads like this: "Published by (your name) at D2D 2023."

This is what IngramSpark says about ISBNs:

"Many self-publishing platforms offer indie authors the opportunity to use a free ISBN. What many authors don't realize is that if you don't purchase the ISBN yourself, your publisher imprint will not be associated with your

book. This means that if you use a free ISBN through a service, it will hold the service's imprint, not your own. Not purchasing an ISBN yourself may also limit where you can print and distribute your own title.

At IngramSpark, we believe it's in your best interest to be recognized as the owner of your work and a publisher in your own right, which is why we encourage publishers to purchase their own ISBNs."

Establish the launch date

Since you are the publisher, you decide the launch date at which time the world will be able to purchase a copy of your book. It will have to be far enough away to enable you to complete all the tasks in the publishing project. This means you have to resist the urge to make the launch date next week! Releasing a book that doesn't yet have a quality book package is self-defeating. It will turn off potential buyers.

So now your job (as the publisher) is to select the launch date. The most important factor to consider is whether or not you will have time to complete all the work involved. Life frequently interferes with this work so the date at this point is an educated guess. But since you are the publisher, you can move the launch date out if you are having trouble making it.

Packager conversion services

In recent developments, print packagers now offer to convert your print book into an ebook, and ebook packagers offer to convert your ebook into a print book.

IngramSpark will convert your print book into an Epub3 compliant ebook, but they will charge you for the service. Currently, the charge is $0.60 per print page. So if your print book has 300 pages the conversion service will cost you $180. You will also have to provide a new, unused ISBN.

Kindle also has conversion services. They will convert a print book to an ebook and an ebook to a print book. Of course, to convert an ebook, you'll have to have a print book cover.

Other packagers most likely offer conversion services as do a number of websites. There is a growth in the number of companies who will convert your manuscript into an ebook, either epub and/or a print book. These companies charge for these services and most are based on a price per manuscript page.

If you decide to use these conversion services, make sure your budget can afford it. And make sure you read all the fine print before making a decision

Step 6: Book blurb

The next four chapters discuss material for your book that must be developed in order to upload it to a packager. However, these four chapters — on book blurbs, description, keywords and categories — are also integral parts of any and all marketing campaigns you will use. Therefore, is in your best interest to invest a large slice of creativity in the development of this material. In other words, don't just slap down the words to get past this chore.

Book blurb

The purpose of the book blurb is to grab the attention of a potential reader. Once you have her attention by means of a great pitch line as the opening sentence, you need to follow that up with a few more sentences that tell her what's different about your book and what's in it for her.

Many new authors consider a book blurb to be a short synopsis. This is a mistake. Book blurbs and a short synopsis are two different animals, and they have very different purposes.

Components

Here are descriptions for each of the three elements involved in a book blurb. Keep the blurb to fewer than a hundred words if possible and no longer than a hundred-fifty words.

Pitch Line: This is the first statement and it is the hook to grab the reader's attention. Its purpose is to persuade the reader to keep reading the other two statements. It should be simple, one or two sentences at most, and it must make a clear statement about your book.

What's in it for the buyer? This is a statement that explains what the reader (i.e. a book buyer) will get in exchange for money. This must be explicit. Tell the reader what benefit he'll get from buying the book. Think of this statement in this way: if your book is surrounded by hundreds of similar-sized books on a shelf in a bookstore or on a web page, what would persuade the buyer to choose your book instead of one of the others?

What's different about this book? With all the books published every month, what makes your book stand out from the others?

The secret to creating an effective blurb is to keep rewriting and condensing it until it expresses the ideas with a minimum of words.

Fiction example

For example, this is the book blurb for my novel *Falstaff's Big Gamble*.

Pitch Line: This novel is Shakespeare's Worst Nightmare.

What's in it for the buyers? It takes two of the Bard's most famous plays, Hamlet and Othello, and recasts them into a fantasy land called Gundarland. There, Hamlet becomes a dwarf and Othello a dark elf

What's different about this book? If that isn't bad enough, these two tragedies are now comedies with Falstaff, Shakespeare's most popular rogue, thrown in as a bonus.

This is the completed blurb:

This novel is Shakespeare's Worst Nightmare. It takes two of the Bard's most famous plays, Hamlet and Othello, and recasts them into a fantasy land called Gundarland. There, Hamlet becomes a dwarf and Othello a dark elf. If that isn't bad enough, these two tragedies are now comedies with Falstaff, Shakespeare's most popular rogue, thrown in as a bonus.

The blurb is only 59 words long.

Non-fiction example

For my non-fiction book, *How to Self-publish and Market a Book*, I developed this blurb.

Pitch Line: Are you planning to self-publish a book? Marketing has to be a vital element of your publishing plan.

What's different about this book? Most books on publishing deal with publishing by itself. Most books on marketing deal with marketing as a stand-alone project. This book combines both publishing and marketing

What's in it for the buyer? This book uniquely combines publishing and marketing into an integrated project.

This is the completed blurb:

Are you planning to self-publish a book? Marketing has to be a vital element of your publishing plan. Most books on publishing deal with publishing by itself. Most books on marketing deal with marketing as a

stand-alone project. This book combines both publishing and marketing. This book uniquely combines publishing and marketing into an integrated project.

The blurb has a total of 57 words.

Using keywords

An attention-grabbing blurb is an important part of your marketing kit. Adding keywords to the blurb makes it even more powerful.

As an example, here is the blurb for my novel The King Who Disappeared before I generated the keywords: *A long time ago, Bohan was a king. But that was before the sleep spell. Now that he's awake again, it's time for revenge.*

The keywords I used are: fantasy adventure, fantasy quest, fantasy humor, fantasy comedy.

Using these keywords, I modified the book blurb to: *A long time ago, at the beginning of this fantasy adventure, Bohan was a king. But that was before the sleep spell. Now that he's awake again, it's time for a quest to get revenge. Fantasy humor doesn't get better than this.*

This increased the word count from 24 words to 42, still fewer than a hundred.

Embedding keywords into your marketing content makes search engines giddy with happiness and they react positively to the experience.

Blurb applications

The initial use for your blurb is as the lead in for the book's description. Make the blurb the first part of the description.

When it comes to marketing the book, the blurb can be used as a social media post, as a teaser with an article about the book and any where you can creatively squeeze it in.

If the entire blurb won't fit, use just the hook line.

Your blurb

Use this format in your notebook to create your blurb. Keep refining, revising and cutting it until you're convinced it's perfect.

Hook (or pitch line):

What's in it for the buyer?

What's different about this book?

Step 7: Description

The book description follows the book blurb on the book's landing page (think Amazon). The term landing page is marketing doublespeak for a sales page or a sell sheet. Together the blurb and description form the most important marketing content your book will have.

The two elements must flow seamlessly together. Any jarring disconnect can send the reader searching for a different book.

Do not use the synopsis as the description. This will be a complete turn-off for book buyers.

Writing a book description for a fiction book is quite different from a non-fiction book.

For fiction

For fiction, the description should attempt to get the visitor interested in the main character and that character's problem. You want the visitor to say to herself, "Oh! I wonder how the character will get out of the mess she's in." Once you get the visitor thinking like that, you're close to getting a sale.

For nonfiction

With a nonfiction book, the goal is to convince the visitor that your book will solve a problem the visitor has. After all, if a visitor landed on your book page, that visitor must have at least a passing interest in the problem.

In addition, you must demonstrate to the visitor that you have the expertise to write the book that will solve her problem

Nonfiction formula

You can use this formula to create your non-fiction book description:
1: Book blurb (include a promise)
2: Book benefits (at least two)
3: Build your authority (why are you an expert on the book's subject?)
4: Describe the contents (don't use the table of contents)
5: Repeat the promise a second time
6: Forceful call to action

This formula was stolen from an excellent article written by Kevin Kruse. Alas, Kruse's web site has disappeared.

Nonfiction example

Using this formula I wrote this description for my book, Creating Stories.

You have a story to tell. Let it out!

Imagine developing a story and telling it in a way that will keep the readers turning the pages.

Hank Quense, the author of more than a dozen highly-regarded novels, shows you how to do it.

In the book, you'll learn how to:
* Develop imagery the reader can use
* Build well-rounded characters the readers will relate to
* Create a path through the plot cloud
* Develop an emotional arc to keep readers on the edge of their seats
* Write dramatic and effective scenes
* Employ story-telling techniques to hold the readers' interest
* And much more

Buy this book now and start telling your story.

Pick up your copy today by clicking on the Buy Now button on the top of the page.

Your description

Write a description for your book. Spend time refining and revising it until it's as perfect as you can make it. Sprinkle in keywords as you go along but don't force them in. Use the keywords only when they fit in naturally.

Step 8: Keywords

Keywords are frequently referred to as tags.

Readers will often search for a book using the name of a best-selling author or the title of a book, but readers can't enter your title or name since you and your book have achieved little recognition. (So far!)

Keyword searches

Another way readers will search for a book is by using a short descriptive phrase such as 'fantasy quest' or 'Regency romance'. This is the situation where you want your book to appear in the search results. To accomplish this, it is vital that you develop a set of keywords that will ensure your book title will show up in the reader's search results.

The keywords you want to use are ones that readers in your genre will use when browsing for a book. These keywords are not necessarily what your book is about: they are the terms a reader will type into a search engine. Let's say your book is a fantasy novel filled with elves and dwarfs. You may think 'dwarfs' and 'elves' would be great keywords. They are not. A reader looking for a fantasy novel won't use them but instead will search on keywords like 'fantasy adventure' or 'fantasy quest.' Consequently, it is important for your marketing efforts that you develop a relevant set of keywords.

Generating keywords

Google has a free keyword planner you can use to help generate your keywords. You can access it using this link: https://ads.google.com/home/tools/keyword-planner/

Another free keyword tool can be found here: https://keywordtool.io/

Here is a trick you can use on Amazon. In the search box, start to type a keyword. Amazon will auto-complete and show you its most popular keywords. As an example, type fantasy into the box. By the time you finish typing 'fantasy' you'll see some keywords that may be relevant. Keep typing and add the word 'adventure'. Now you'll see better keyword suggestions.

Number of keywords

Draft2Digital has no limit on the number of keywords you can use for your book while Kindle limits you to seven keywords. It is in your best interest to develop at least seven keywords. More is better.

Keyword uses

What are keywords used for? Once you get a set of keywords, you can use them in a variety of ways. Besides the packagers and blog posts, you can embed them into your book blurb, your book description and your short and long synopses. Search engines love this usage. Keywords are also useful as hashtags in social media posts

Step 9: Categories

When you upload your book to a packager, you'll have to select categories for it. You'll be allowed to select two different categories from a bewildering assortment of choices.

Your book is ranked against other books within the same category. Ranking high in a category is a good way to increase sales.

Kindle Direct Publishing (KDP) Categories

This is what Kindle says about categories:

Categories are the sections of the Amazon site where customers can find your book. Think of browse categories like the sections of a physical bookstore (fiction, history, and so on). During title setup, you'll choose two Browse Categories from a list. This list is based on the BISAC (Book Industry Standards and Communications) code. We use the two categories you choose, along with your selected keywords, to place your book into Amazon categories.

Category lists

This link will give a complete list of all categories and sub-categories:
https://www.thriftbooks.com/sitemap/

Selecting categories

Selecting your categories is a confusing situation, but it is important. To provide some more guidance, here are links to two articles on the subject.
https://blog.reedsy.com/guide/kdp/amazon-book-categories/

https://kindlepreneur.com/how-to-choose-the-best-kindle-ebook-kdp-category/

Step 10: Price

How do you come up with a price for your book? I'll answer that in a moment. First, a few words of advice. Don't let your ego get in the way of making a rational decision on this subject. It's true you may have spent years producing this masterpiece, and you think the book's value is enormous and that thousands of readers will be happy to pay a premium price to get a chance to own their very own copy. Well, you're wrong. You are an unknown author and unknown authors can't command premium prices. It'll be hard enough selling your book without the added burden of an unrealistically high price.

Print books

Let's consider print books first. The best place to do this research is on Amazon or some other major book site, although you can do this in a bookstore or even a library. Once on the site, search for books that are similar to yours. If your book is non-fiction and covers plumbing repairs, search for other plumbing repair books. Note the price for the ones that have similar subject matter and a similar number of pages. That is the target price of your book. If your research reveals four similar print books and their prices range from $15.99 to $24.99, your book should be priced somewhere within that range. You can also make a pricing decision to make your book available at a lower price if you wish.

If your book is fiction, search for other books within your genre. This may be a tougher job than with nonfiction books. Genre books have superstar authors who command premium prices. Ignore them. You don't have the clout to demand a premium price — yet. Your search should be for lesser known authors in your genre. If your book has three-hundred pages, you should search for other similar genre books with three-hundred pages, approximately. Comparing your three-hundred page book to a six-hundred page one isn't very productive. The six-hundred page print book will cost more to produce because of the larger number of pages and subsequent production costs, so that book will require a higher price than a three-hundred page print book. Set your price to get the best possible sales at your current status as a new author.

Ebook prices

For an ebook, the search process is similar but you'll probably come up with a confusing array of data. A bit of explanation is in order. There is a debate going on about ebook pricing. Many voices claim that ebooks sell best if they're priced at $0.99. Others contend that a higher price yields more profits but fewer sales. There are studies that conclude the sweet spot for an ebook is $2.99 to $5.99. Obviously, an ebook selling for $2.99 will bring in more revenue for an author than an ebook selling at $0.99. On the other hand, an ebook selling for $.99 could sell more books than a higher priced ebook. You can ask for advice on web sites like LinkedIn and you'll get replies, many of them contradictory. After reading the replies, it still comes down to you making a decision. Make sure this is a business decision.

Another complicating factor is the presence of best-selling authors. Their ebooks come from the major publishing houses. Their price will be closer to $10.00 or even higher. It will not even be close to $.99. Here again, the premium price is due to name recognition and clout. If you price your ebook close to $10.00 you won't have to worry about tracking sales; you won't get any. A first-time self-published author simply can't expect to use premium pricing and sell any books, no matter how great the content is.

Fiction ebooks are very sensitive to price. The books are selling entertainment and readers will compare prices before making a buy decision. That's why your ebooks can't compete with well-known authors on price.

Nonfiction ebooks are not as sensitive. Most nonfiction books provide a solution to a problem. If the reader sees the book as a way to solve her problem, she won't be as concerned about the price.

Print books are far less sensitive to price concerns although it is possible to price your book out of consideration.

My pricing strategy

Here is my pricing strategy. For my novels, I start out at $3.99 for ebook and $19.99 for print. As the book ages, I'll drop the ebook price lower.

For nonfiction, I initially price a multi-topic ebook at $5.49. For nonfiction print books, I'll price them at $21.99

Some of my nonfiction books are dedicated to a smaller topic (like Publishing Insights) and I'll price them at $2.99 or even $1.49 depending on the size of the book.

Marketing

Table of contents
Book marketing equation.   131
Book marketing basics.   132
Strategic planning.   132
Landing page.   134
Author platform.   136
Book reviews.   140
Giveaways.   142
Consignments   144
In person selling.   145
Social media marketing.   147
Targeting.   147
Social media posts and ads   149
Promotion sites.   152
Experts and Authors.   154

Book marketing equation

By way of introducing this section on marketing, let me show you the equation that sums it all up:

$$SBM = ((QBP + \Sigma R + E_{sub(lp)} + \Sigma(A + P) + E_{subM} + \Sigma SM))L$$

where:
SBM stands for Successful Book Marketing
QBP means Quality Book Package
Σr is the summation of all book reviews
$E_{sub(lp)}$ stands for the effectiveness of book's Landing Page
P is for Promotions
A is for Ads
(A + P) means the summation of all results for ads and promotions
E_{subM} is for email
ΣSM means the accumulation of all your social media effectiveness
L stands for the Luck Factor (note: Luck can be a negative number)

This equation is one of the more useless pieces of information you'll ever come across but it rather nicely illustrates the complexity of the situation. Simply put, book marketing is a tricky project involving a lot of disparate moving parts. Once you accumulate all these components in the equation and mix in a bit of luck, you're on your way to a successful marketing campaign.

Book marketing basics

Strategic planning

The Strategic Marketing Plan is the master plan for all your marketing activities, and it directs all the tactical tasks that you decide to use. If this sounds nebulous, let me rephrase it. All the marketing tasks except the strategic plan are tactical ones. All these tactical tasks add up to build your tactical plan. Your tactical plan must be in agreement with the objectives in your strategic plan. If the tactical plans and the strategic plan don't agree, some of your marketing activities will be a waste of time and will possibly also waste money. A marketing task shouldn't be used just because it's doable or easy; it should be used because it agrees with the strategic plan.

Marketing plans

The initial thing you need to know about marketing a book is that it can't be a half-hearted effort involving an occasional email or blog post, stuff you send out when you don't have anything better to do. You have to dedicate a chunk of time, effort and, yes, money to market the book.

Product, customers, competitors

These questions will require thinking on your part. The answers are not always apparent.

Describe the book.
- What's different about the book?
- What benefit does the customer get from buying your book?
- Why would a customer buy your book instead of a competitor's book?
- Who are your competitors?
- What benefits do they offer?
- How is your book better than the competitor's book?

- Who are your target customers?
- What sales channels will you use to sell your book?
- What marketing channels will you use to reach your targeted customers?
- What will your book be priced at?
- How does your price compare to the competitor's price?

Objectives and budgets
- What are the financial objectives for this plan?
- How will you measure these financial results?
- What are the secondary objectives for this plan?
- How will you measure the results?
- What is your marketing budget for year 1?
- What is your marketing budget for year 2?

Customer identification

Once you identify the customer, list the sites where those customers can be reached. List as many as possible in your notebook.

Site 1:

Site 2:

Site 3:

Site 4:

Site 5:

Site 6:

Landing page

The landing page is where the sale is clinched or lost. Social media marketing is designed to only deliver visitors to that landing page. That's all it does.

So, it stands to reason that the landing page is where you have to invest your maximum creativity. If you have a publisher, it will create a landing page for your book. If you self-publish, the landing page is your job. You have to write the page elements before you upload the book to the packager. You can also revise and strengthen it after it is published.

Social media

This diagram shows the operation of social media marketing.

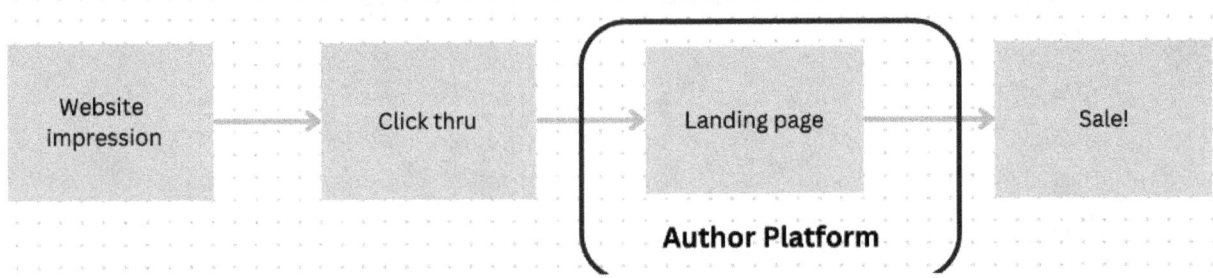

An ad campaign consists of a paid ad on a promotional site. It can also be a post on a Facebook business account or a tweet or a number of other things.

Whatever the post is, it consists of some words and usually a graphic. It also has a built-in link to the book's landing page. So let's say you pay for a Facebook ad. Facebook will show the post on people's pages. That's called an impression.

If someone sees the impression and is curious, they will click on the post and the built-in link will open the landing page. This action is called a Click Thru. The percentage of impressions that result in a click thru is known as the Click thru rate or CTR.

So if your post is shown a 1,000 times and you see that you have a CTR of 1%, that means ten people visited the landing page by clicking on an impression. Does that mean you sold ten books? Probably not, but you may have sold some books because of this.

Landing page components

The components, in the order an Amazon visitor sees them, are:
1. The cover
2. The ratings
3. The price
4. The blurb
5. The description

Any one of these components can drive a visitor away. If the components all mesh together, the visitor may be convinced to buy the book.

The components listed are described in detail under Publishing and won't be repeated here. They are all part publishing and part marketing.

Author platform

The landing page is about your book. The author platform is about you, the author.

The platform is how you introduce your self to the world and consists of a number of components that have to be developed and kept updated.

Platform components

Your author platform, at a minimum, consists of the following components.
- Signature (Sig) files
- Author website
- Media kit
- Author Central page
- Social media accounts

Sig files

Sig files, short for signature files, are a cute way to remind people about your website and your books. It's part author platform and part marketing.

Sig files aren't hard to create but you'll have to do some digging because every email program does it different. Look under the general information tab or search for signatures on the email program.

These are my current sig files.

hank quense
Amazon page
Novels
Writers & authors resource center

They link to three different sites that I want people to visit.

Author website

You need a website of some sort. It's a place to post blogs and have a second landing page. It can also host your media kit to be downloaded. It can use Wordpress app or some other app and it doesn't need a lot of sophisticated features.

It provides a second landing page for your book, so don't skimp on this aspect of the website. Make this landing page as great as the original one.

Media kit

The purpose of a media kit is to let folks in the media and other interested parties know about your writing credentials. If the book is your only writing project so far, there won't be a lot of material, but start it anyway. If you have published short stories, articles or other content, add it to plump up your résumé. The media kit lives on your website or blog and must be available to anyone who wants to download it. For that reason, you may want to consider not putting personal information in it like your home address or your phone number.

So, what goes into a media kit? Here is a list of items that make up your kit:

- Bio.
- Press releases.
- Website links.
- Body of work.
- Book descriptions.
- Book reviews.

Make sure the media kit is a doc or pdf file so it can be downloaded and opened by everyone.

As long as we're discussing the media kit contents, it's a good time to write your bio. Write two bios, a long version of one or more pages and a short one, a single paragraph or two. The long one goes in the media kit, and the short one can be used in guest posts on blogs and in other places.

Bios are written in the third person, not first person. Include your photo in the bio and make sure it's a good picture. Preferably, you should be smiling. Don't use a picture in which you are frowning, glaring, snarling or otherwise looking unfriendly or hostile. You don't want to scare away potential customers.

Author central

This is how Amazon helps authors sell books. After all when you sell books, their revenue increases. One way Amazon helps is by allowing you to establish an author page.

Once your book is available for sale or pre-order on Amazon, you can start an Author Page. If you have a publisher, it may (or may not) have started your author central page.

Once you establish the page, you can add a lot more content to the book's landing page that you couldn't do when you uploaded the manuscript to the packager. Take advantage of this great marketing tool.

Social media accounts

Social media is a bit controversial since it means different things to different people. It's also difficult to define because it has so many different facets. However, it is essential that you sign up with a few social media accounts. Which ones are up to you. Different sites will resonate with different people.

Another important topic is how you construct the social media posts. I'll show a few different ones and describe their usefulness.

- WWW.something.com. If the link in this post is for the landing page, it won't get any clicks because it doesn't tell the reader anything. Many readers will think it downloads malware and will avoid it.
- *Check it out!* WWW.something.com. This one is slightly better. It has a Call to Action, but few will click on it for the same reason mentioned in the first post.
- *Check it out!* WWW.something.com *#romance #humor*. This one is much better because it adds a few hashtags to tell the reader what the link is about. (More on hashtags a bit later).
- *Check it out! (Hook line from blurb)* WWW.something.com *#romance #humor (cover image)*. This one is the best. It tells the reader a bit more and offers a hint of what they'll find at the link. It also contains an image. Images attract attention. Book covers are ideal to use. This one may get people to visit the landing page.
- *Check it out! (Blurb video)* WWW.something.com *#romance #humor (cover image)*. This one is also good, and video attracts a lot of attention.

Hashtags

An important part of social media is hashtags. These are words or phrases preceded by a #. Hashtags are social media talk for keywords. You can add one or two hashtags (or more) to your post so people interested in that hashtag can find it. If you click on a hashtag in a post, you'll see a list of current posts on that subject.

Some of the hashtags I use are:

#fantasy

#scifi

#humor

#satire

#amwriting

#publishing

#selfpublishing

#bookmarketing

There are many, many more hashtags you can employ. The great thing about hashtags is that it expands the number of people who will see your post.

Book reviews

Book reviews are probably the best sales and marketing tool you can have besides a great landing page. Granted, reviews aren't easy to get, but they are worth the effort.

There is no such thing as having too many reviews. They tell a landing page visitors that other readers liked the book. That eliminates the suspicion that the visitor may be getting tricked into buying a piece a junk. You can get reviews on your own, through review sites and by buying them.

On your own

Every author does a bit of this. You contact your relatives and friends and ask them to read and review your new book. Another approach is to send out social media posts asking for contacts to review the book. This is quite iffy. Many of the contacts who respond have no intention of ever writing a review: they are simply after a free book. Still, you will get an occasional review this way.

Review sites

There are many sites that will, for a fee, spread the word about your book to their list of potential reviewers. Many of these sites will only promote ebooks on Kindle. Of those sites, many will only promote ebooks that are heavily discounted. Others will only accept ebooks that are free. Note that any reviews that come out of these promotions are not paid reviews. The fee does not buy a review: rather you're paying for access to the site's list of potential reviewers.

You can find many of these sites by running a search for them. When you land on such a site, make sure you read ALL the fine print.

Paid reviews

Sites such as Publishers Weekly and Kirkus Reviews will review your book for a fee. A large fee. Amazon will not allow paid reviews to be posted for your book. These reviews can, however, be added to the book's content using the Amazon Central Page feature.

Midwest Book Review is a review site that is much less costly. Go to https://www.midwestbookreview.com to learn more. There are many more paid sites than these two, but they are not always prestigious so your money doesn't really buy anything valuable.

A necessary chore

While getting more reviews can be a frustrating and time-consuming chore, it's an essential task in an author's basic marketing plans.

Giveaways

One way to gain readers is to give away copies of your book. Giveaways are different from running an ad promoting a book that is free. Giveaways are much more targeted.

There are a number of reasons to run a giveaway. Firstly, some of these readers may post a review. Secondly, the giveaway may enable you to grow your list of emails. Thirdly, it increases your name recognition. Finally, it can lead to future sales.

Print and ebook

If you give away a print book, you'll incur both production and postage costs in getting the books from the packager, and then you'll have more postage costs when you send it out. If you give away an ebook, it doesn't cost you anything. Ebooks don't have production costs and they don't have postage requirements. However, print book giveaways will attract more interest, especially if you sign the book with the reader's name.

Random drawings

You can write a blog post stating that you're giving away X copies of your new book in a random drawing to people who sign up via an email form. You can use many emailer sites for this effort.   At the end of the signup period, select the winners and attach the ebook to an email. Ask the winners to write a review if they enjoy the book. Spread the word about your giveaway on Twitter, Facebook, LinkedIn and wherever else you have accounts.

Raffles

You can commission an online raffle using a site like Rafflecopter: https://www.rafflecopter.com. This site has a paid monthly subscription plan. Sign up for it if you plan to run a lot of raffles, otherwise use its free trial offer. Use your social media accounts to promote the raffle.

Freebies

If you have your book on D2D, you can change the price of the book to a free download and run this sale for a limited period of time. Promote the freebie using social media.

If you have your book on Kindle and it's enrolled in Kindle Select, you can offer your book for free five days in every quarter. Promote the offer using social media.

Consignments

Consignment selling means the bookstore will take copies of the book, but the store will not order them. They will only accept copies of the book that you order and pay for. This relieves the bookstore from initially paying for the books and handling returns later on. In other words, it improves their cashflow and transfers inventory management to the author.

Consignment deals
Under consignment deals, the bookstore will keep a percentage of all book sales and the author gets what's left. Typically, the bookstore will want 25% to 40% of the sale revenue.

A consignment deal typically will last three to six months. At the end of the period, you settle the payment issue and walk away with the unsold books under your arm and a check in your pocket. If some books were sold, the bookstore may agree to renew the deal.

Consignment contracts
Consignment selling requires a contract that is signed by the author and the store. The contract will contain the book title, number of books in the deal, the book price and the store's percentage of sales.

You can find blank contracts at a number of websites including Legalzoom: https://www.legalzoom.com and Rocketlawyer: https://www.rocketlawyer.com

Book display
There is one thing to keep in mind with consignment deals: ask whether your book will be displayed on a shelf where people can see it or will it be dumped in the storage room where no one will ever see it. If your books are slated to go into storage, you may want to rethink the consignment deal.

In person selling

It's the 21st century and most book marketing and selling occurs via the internet. Nevertheless, there are marketing and sales opportunities the old fashioned way: in person.

Physical book selling

Bookstores are a tough nut to crack for self-published authors, especially if it's a first book and the author has no name recognition. Most bookstores in this country use Ingram as their distributor. If your book is distributed by Ingram, is returnable and has the industry standard discount (55%), there is a chance bookstores will order your book and put it on their shelves for a while. However, bookstores will not know about the book's existence unless you tell them about it. Contacting bookstores one at a time is a mind-numbing activity, especially if you pursue out-of-area and out-of-state bookstores. The only cost-effective way to query these stores is by using email.

Just because your book isn't on a shelf in a bookstore doesn't mean the store can't order a copy if a customer requests one. Barnes & Noble and other bookstores can order a print copy of the book just by entering the ISBN or the book title into their computer system. Within a few days, the book will arrive ready to be picked up by the customer who ordered it.

If your print book packager is Kindle, there is no, nada, zippo, zilch, not-a-prayer of the book store ordering a copy of the book to put on its shelves. Kindle will not allow returns, and that is a deal breaker as far as the book store is concerned. Although the bookstore won't put the Kindle book on its shelves, it can and will order a copy if a customer requests it.

Libraries

Most libraries rely primarily on Baker & Taylor as their distributor, but they will also use Ingram. If your book isn't distributed by one of these two companies, you have very little chance of getting the book onto library shelves unless you give them a free copy.

Once you get the book into a library (start with your local ones), ask if they will arrange a book reading and signing. A library may be more receptive to the signing than a bookstore will be. They'll usually put a blurb into the local paper, thus increasing your exposure. Make sure you have a supply of books to sell. This should be a budget item that you fund if you have a print edition of your book.

Some libraries may want a slice of revenue if they allow you to sell books at the reading. My experience is they'll want ten percent of whatever you make. I think it's a great deal. Libraries need all the financial help they can get.

Book events

Book events are gatherings such as book fairs where readers go to peruse tables staffed by authors and loaded with their books. These are usually run by libraries, at least around where I live. Of course, these are difficult to get involved with if you only have ebooks.

Other book events are street fairs and flea markets. In these you may have to rent a table from the event's organizers. That means for you to make a profit on the event, you first have to sell enough books to cover the cost of the table.

Social media marketing

Targeting

Targeting is a marketing concept that refers to limiting who sees an ad or a campaign. With proper targeting the ad is only seen by people who have an interest in the subject of the ad.

Without proper targeting, the ad is seen primarily by people who have no interest in the subject of the ad. In other words, the result of improper targeting is to waste money.

General population
The vast majority of the general population has no interest in your book. Only a small sliver who likes your genre will have an interest in the book. Reaching the tiny sliver shown in the graphic is the objective of social media marketing.

Focusing an ad campaign on that sliver is the only way an ad can be effective. The more of the general population that sees the ad, the more money is wasted and the less effective the ad is.

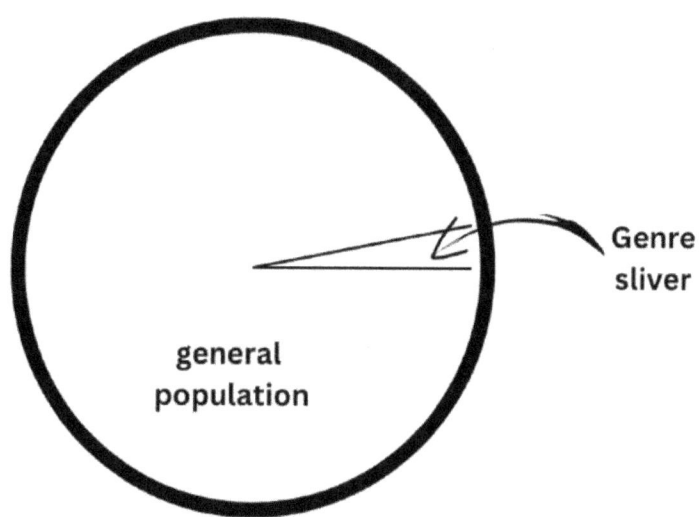

Fiction and nonfiction

These two different types of books have different targeting requirements.

Fiction is targeted at the genre of the book, such as romance, scifi, mystery, etc. This type of targeting should also be used for memories and creative nonfiction since they are telling stories and have a genre also.

Nonfiction has to be targeted towards the problem the book is addressing such as plumbing leaks or kitchen remodeling. This type of targeting can rely more on demographics than the fiction books will.

Demographic targeting

This type of targeting aims at segments of the population. In the case of plumbing problems and kitchen remodeling, one segment would be homeowners. Since teenagers don't usually own homes, age demographics would exclude the teenage group.

YA novels on the other hand, definitely have to target teenagers.

Kids' picture books are NOT targeted at kids. Children don't have money or credit cards and don't scroll through the web looking for books to buy. Kids' books are targeted at parents and grandparents

Social media posts and ads

Let's talk about how social media ads work. This is an important concept and you should have a clear understanding about it. The key fact here is that the social media ads, posts, campaigns, etc. do NOT sell any books. The function of the social media activity is to deliver visitors to the book's landing page. Here's the graphic you saw previously.

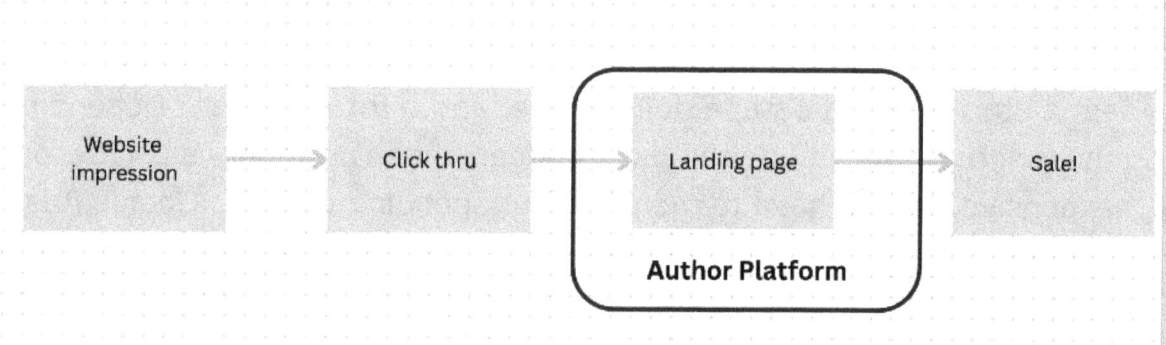

Posts

Posts such as you find on Facebook are for your friends and family. Constantly posting about your book there will drive people away from your feed. This type of marketing will result in few if any sales. Posts that read, "Buy my book, please?" do not accomplish anything useful.

How ads work

Almost all social media sites will allow you to buy ads for your book. Some ads are simple and others are complex. Here are a few generalities about how ads work.

There are several different types of promotions. In one, you pay a flat fee to promote your book. With these, you fill in text boxes with the title, description, price, buy links and the cover. The site converts the text boxes into a document, sends it out in an email or newsletter and (hopefully) people buy a copy of the book.

Other promotions are more complicated. First, you have to construct the ad. This usually consists of the book cover or the title and a very short sentence followed by a call-to-action (i.e., Buy Now!) and a link to a site selling your book. The cost of the ad is a variable. In one version, you pay per thousand impressions. An impression is your ad showing up on some website or webpage. You hope the ad results in viewers clicking on it. When they do, they are taken to a page selling your book. Typical prices are a dollar or two per thousand impressions and are usually fixed by the promotional site.

In a second version, you pay a fee every time someone clicks on your ad but you aren't charged by the number of impressions. In these ads, the cost may be twenty-five or fifty cents per click. The fee can also be higher or lower. In most cases, you set the price you are willing to pay.

With either version, you construct the ad using a set of options. You can set a start and end date, a daily budget and a total budget. Depending on the length of the ad and the daily budget, these promotions can become expensive, so you have to monitor your spending closely. Google Ads (formerly Adwords) is typical of this type of promotional site. The success of these ad campaigns hinges on the keywords you select for the ad. Google has tools to help you select the correct ones.

With the reports for these ad campaigns, you'll come across a metric called CTR or Click Through Rate. If your ad was shown 200 times and two people clicked on it, you had a CTR of 1%. That sounds bad doesn't it? Actually, a CTR of 1% is very good since major corporations only get a 3 to 4% CTR. Remember, most people are not interested in whatever you are peddling, so expect a low CTR.

The third — very expensive — kind of promotion involves hiring a promotion company to promote your book. These promotions will require you to sign a contract and pay up front. In return, the company will do an enormous amount of work promoting your book. Since there are large amounts of money involved here, make sure you do a lot of research before signing up with such a company. LinkedIn may be a good place to start your research. Another site that can connect you to promotion companies is https://www.bark.com. There is a lot of stuff on this site, you may have to scroll around to find what you need.

Before committing to this type of promotion, ensure that it will target your genre and not the general public.

Facebook pages

Facebook encourages you to start a "page" for your book. Pages are different from the regular posts you use to share news and pictures with your friends and family. Pages are for your business.

Over time, you may accumulate a lot of followers and that is good. But it isn't as good as you may think it is. Let's say you have 250 followers for your page. You put a post on the page announcing a new limited time discount on your book. You may be shocked to learn that only a handful of followers will see the post. Perhaps as few as ten (or less!) will see it. What happened to all the other followers? Facebook will gladly show the post to more followers if you 'boost' the post. Boosting involves throwing money at Facebook.

Alas, it isn't only Facebook who does this. All social media sites I know of do this.

Book Promotion sites

This topic is not about the typical social media ads such as you can commission on Facebook, Twitter and other sites.

The resources listed here are book promotional sites where you can pay a fee and the sites will send out an email to its contacts telling them about your book. Other sites will do something different to tell a fraction of the world about your book.

There are many, many of these sites. Some will only handle books on Kindle that have been discounted to $.99 or that are free for a time or permanently.

Some sites will charge a large fee and will engage in a lot more activity than sending out an email.

There are too many promotional sites to list them all or even to enumerate the types of sites. In this topic I'll identify a few of them to give you a feel for the different sites. You'll have to do research to find out more about the many sites.

Site listing

Promotional websites pop up continuously, and a web search will give you a list of sites to check on. Here is a link to a webpage that lists a hundred or more book promotion sites: https://www.readersintheknow.com/list-of-book-promotion-sites. The list contains a few sites that no longer exist. Perform your due diligence in going through the list.

Scams

Then there are promotional sites which are nothing but scams. It is in your best interest to read all the fine print before you commit money to a promotional site that looks suspicious. What does suspicious mean? For starters, if a site guarantees a certain number of book sales, it most certainly is suspicious. Before you commit money to any promotion site that hasn't been recommended to you, ask about it on your LinkedIn and Goodreads groups.

Another scam is a site that guarantees X number of 5 star ratings for your book. The ratings will occur but they are from people who haven't read the book. Getting 25 5-star ratings in a single day looks very suspicious. The ratings won't be on Amazon. They will be on sites like Goodreads.

Bookbub

https://www.bookbub.com/launch is a big site that has two types of promotions: very expensive email lists and pay per click. Their email lists are extensive and Bookbub is very selective about whom they allow to advertise, even if you're willing to pay the fee. You can submit your book free of charge and you'll be informed if it's selected or not. If your book is selected, you pay the fee (think a minimum of $800 or $900 dollars: it keeps going up!) The higher the price of your book during the promotion, the greater the fee. If selected, you will sell a lot of books. Will it cover the cost of the campaign? I don't know, that is impossible to predict. I've used this type of ad several times in the past, but that was when Bookbub first started out and the fee was a hundred bucks or so. The site became wildly successful, the prices shot through the roof and it became very tough to get selected.

Bookbub also has pay-per-click campaigns you can use.

Amazon Marketing Services (AMS)

Once your book is on Amazon, you can use its Amazon Marketing Services (AMS) https://advertising.amazon.com. Amazon has several options available, including pay-per-click and other types of ad campaigns.

The key to using these types of ads is to initiate many simultaneous ads using a number of different keywords. This also applies to Bookbub and Google ads. Since you pay per click, having a lot of ads doesn't necessarily increase your costs. If the keyword doesn't attract much notice, it won't be clicked and you won't be charged. The idea behind this scheme is that the more keywords you use, the more likely one of them will be seen by an interested party.

Experts and authors

Facebook, Twitter and other social media sites allow an author to run sales campaigns. The campaigns are restricted to people who use that site. Those people are shown an ad (called an impression). Facebook charges by the number of impressions, not clicks, and this means the charges mount up quickly. Facebook also doesn't have a budget cut-off. Your ad will run until you manually stop it. If you don't monitor the ad, you will end up owing Facebook a huge amount of money.

Social media targeting

One huge problem with social media campaigns (for authors) is that it is next to impossible to target the tiny sliver of people who would be interested in the genre of the book. Keep in mind that authors are only a small fraction of all the companies, corporations and individuals who use social media marketing. All of these can more accurately target their customers than authors can.

To summarize, authors use social media marketing campaigns at their own risk.

How the big kids do it

Large companies spend millions of dollars on social media marketing and are successful at it. Why is that? Because they have SEO experts and social media marketing experts on staff, and those experts make sure the campaigns are successful. (SEO stands for search engine optimization.)

Consequently, when these companies run a campaign, it precisely targets the customers, the SEO is exact and the copy and graphics are professionally created.

How authors do it

When authors create a social media campaign, the SEO is a guess if it's considered at all, the graphics and copy may be suitable, but the targeting is also a guess or a vague compromise. Authors, in other words, are rank amateurs and risk throwing money away on sales campaigns that are most likely doomed from the start.

SEO

Search Engine Optimization is a complex subject that requires a lot of study and work to master. Mastering SEO is not the stuff that authors want to do. Authors want to write books, not take college level courses to understand the intricacies of SEO.

If you do a web search on SEO, you'll uncover a ton of articles "explaining" how to use SEO. Most of the articles will display a to-do list for effective SEO usage. Unfortunately, the to-do list will be exactly that: a list of items to work on without any clue as to how to implement each item

What should authors do?

Instead of throwing money away on social media ads, hire an expert who can be either an individual or a company.

This can be a major expense but, in the long run, it may be cheaper than running your own ads on social media. This can also result in higher sales than the do-it-yourself approach. https://www.bark.com can be used to find a suitable company that will use its expertise to promote your book. Using this approach, research the site or individual and read ALL of the fine print.

Unfortunately, this advice also runs into problems. This time the problem is the "experts" who talk a great game but don't deliver the goods. There are sites and individuals who claim marketing expertise but really don't possess it. How can you tell? Ask around. Perhaps other authors know something about the site you're thinking about using.

Another issue is hiring the wrong expert. Perhaps, in this case, you want to promote your book but the site's expertise is in promoting a different product and consequently doesn't have a book buying clientele.

What this situation comes down to is this: It is the author's responsibility to research the site or expert under consideration to ensure the money spent won't be a waste of resources.

Index

Foreword   7

Planning.   11
Fiction planning
Initial details
Outline
Cast of characters
Character development
Plot
Typical plot sequence
Setting
World building
But, what if...

Fiction writing workshop   14
Lesson 1: Getting Started
- Target audience
- Ideas
- Writing prompts
- Story definition
- Story ideas
- How many words?
- Assignment 1

Lesson 2: Setting
- Imagery
- Setting
- Assignment 2

Lesson 3: Character development
- Characters
- Physical attributes
- Biography
- Mental attributes
- Dreams
- Memories
- Mirages
- Philosophy
- Dominant reader emotion
- Antagonist development

- Assignment 3

Lesson 4: Character arc
- Character arc
- Examples
- Assignment 4

Lesson 5: Plots
- Plots
- Plot problem
- Bad news
- Plot cloud
- Plot development
- Constructing a plot
- Generic plot path
- Successive failures
- Conflict
- Assignment 5

Lesson 6: Subplots
- Subplot uses
- Subplot example
- More subplot stuff
- Nesting
- Assignment 6

Lesson 7: Scene design
- Scene design
- Optional requirements
- Scene goal
- Emotional arc
- Assignment 7

Lesson 8: Emotional arc
- Emotional arc
- Example
- Plot & emotional arcs-1
- Plot & Emotional arcs-2
- Plot & Emotional arcs-3
- Assignment 8

Lesson 9: Point of view
- Point of view
- Omniscient POV
- Third person limited POV
- First person POV
- POV examples
- Assignment 9

Lesson 10: Story-telling techniques

- Tense
- Stimulus and reactions
- Foreshadowing
- Show don't tell

Dialog and exposition
Assignment 10
Lesson 11: Dialog
- Who is telling the story
- Formatting
- Must be realistic
- Dialog, not conversation
- Realistic talking
- Assignment 11
- *Lesson 12: Assorted topics*

Central metaphor
Crisis management
Adverbs
Empty words
Assignment 12
Lesson 13: Wrapping it all up
- Putting it all together
- Writing apps
- Miscellaneous stuff
- Assignment 13

Author business   64
Starting a business
- Think like a CEO
- What type of business
- Sole proprietorship
- Limited liability corporation'
- Employer Identification number (EIN)
- Resources

Payments
- Royalty splits: ebooks
- Royalty splits: print books
- Royalty splits: audio books

Keeping track
- Revenue and expense
- Profit and loss
- Budgets

Taxes
- Taxes and breathing

- Schedule C
- Hobby or business?
- Selling print books

Breaking even
- Overview
- Breakeven templates
- Example
- Analysis
- Implications

Start a publishing company
- What?
- Pros and cons
- Pros
- Cons
- Book publisher associations

Resources
- Links
- Books

Publishing   89
Publishing overview.
- Manuscript status
- Time frames
- Lack of commonality
- What type of book?
- Comparison list
- Useful links
- Publishing options

Traditional publishing
- Submission package
- Query cover letter
- Synopsis
- Agents
- Agent queries
- Publishers

Self-publishing action plan
Self-publishing tidbits
- Common self-publishing misconceptions
- Bring on demand (POD)
- Preorders
- Publishing budgets
- Publishing task list

Step 1: Editing
- Professional editing
- Four types of editors
- Editing
- More on editing

Step 2: Covers
- Covers in general
- Pre-made covers
- Print covers
- Print cover spines
- Print book size

Step 3: Formatting
- Print book formatting
- Ebook formatting
- Epub3 requirements
- Ebook table of contents
- Embedded links
- Other help

Step 4: Book design
- Bring book size
- Fonts
- Line spacing
- Headers & Footers
- Cheat sheets

Step 5: Packagers
- Kindle
- Draft2Digital
- IngramSpark
- Getting paid
- ISBN
- Establish the launch date
- Packager conversion services

Step 6: Book blurb
- Book blurb
- Components
- Fiction example
- Non-fiction example
- Using keywords
- Blurb applications
- Your blurb

Step 7: Description
- For fiction
- For non-fiction'

- Non-fiction example
- Your description

Step 8: Keywords
- Keyword searches
- Generating keywords
- Number of keywords
- Keyword uses

Step 9: Categories
- KDP categories
- Category lists
- Selecting categories

Step 10: Price
- Print books
- Ebook prices
- My pricing strategy

Marketing 130
Book marketing equation
Book marketing basics
Strategic planning
- Marketing plans
- Product, customers, competitors
- Customer identification

Landing pages
- Social media
- Landing page components

Author Platform
- Platform components
- Sig files
- Author website
- Media kit
- Author central
- Social media accounts
- Hashtags

Book reviews
- On your own
- Review sites
- Paid reviews
- A necessary chore

Giveaways
- Print and ebook
- Random drawings

- Raffles

Consignments
- Consignment deals
- Consignment contracts
- Book display

In person selling
- Physical book selling'
- Libraries
- Book events
- Book signings

Social media marketing
Targeting
- General population
- Fiction and non-fiction
- Demographic targeting

Social media posts
- Posts
- How ads work
- Facebook pages

Promotion sites
- Site listing
- Scams
- Bookbub
- Amazon marketing services

Experts and authors
- Social media targeting
- How the big kids do it
- How authors do it
- SEO
- What should authors do?

About the Author

Hank Quense writes humorous and satiric sci-fi and fantasy stories. He also writes and lectures about fiction writing, self-publishing, book marketing and author business. He has published 21 books and 50 short stories along with dozens of articles. His two daughters and five grandchildren live in nearby towns.

Other books by Hank Quense

Fiction:
Gundarland Stories
Tales From Gundarland
Falstaff's Big Gamble
Wotan's Dilemma
The King Who Disappeared
Princess Moxie Series
Moxie's Problem
Moxie's Decision
Queen Moxie

Non-fiction:
Creating Stories
How to Self-publish and Market a Book
Book Marketing Fundamentals
Business Basics for Authors
Fiction Writing Workshops for Kids
Self-publish a Book in 10 Steps
Infographic Guide to Creating Stories
Infographic Guide to Mind-mapping a Novel

You can find all of these books at https://www.amazon.com/~/e/B002BM76IE.

Links
You want links? Here you go:

Writers And Authors Resource Center:

https://hankquense.podia.com/

Hank's Facebook fiction page:
https://www.facebook.com/StrangeWorldsOnline?ref=hl

Twitter: https://twitter.com/hanque99

LinkedIn: https://www.linkedin.com/in/hanque/

Goodreads: https://www.goodreads.com/author/show/3002079.Hank_Quense

Bookbub: https://www.bookbub.com/authors/hank-quense

www.ingramcontent.com/pod-product-compliance
Lightning Source LLC
LaVergne TN
LVHW081547070526
838199LV00061B/4245